I AM
Alpha and Omega
The Beginning and The End

A commentary on Biblical History & Predictions
by

DAVID B HATHCOCK

David B Hathcock, Author
DavidHath@msn.com
1-864-225-1738

Other books by
David B Hathcock

Tumbleweed
Louisiana Heart
Biblical Symbolism 2
He touched me
The Eternal Purpose
Ring That Bell
Ages
Revelation Simplified
Tanniyn
Whiteskins
We Are Warriors

Hebrews 5:12

For when for the time ye ought to be teachers, ye have need that one teaches you again which be the first principles of the oracles of God; and are become such as have need of milk, and not of strong meat.

Revelation 1:8

(8) I am Alpha and Omega, the beginning, and the ending, saith the Lord, which is, and which was, and which is to come, the Almighty.

Chapter One

Why are we here?

Of course, the correct answer is, "we were born here". But were you? O', I know your physical body was born here; but, what about the real you? You know, the person you were before you were placed inside the physical or flesh body you now use to get around on your daily endeavors? You didn't know you had two bodies? Surprise, surprise?

As the apostle Paul put it and described this phenomenal so well in 1 Corinthians 15:42-54 as given below.

(42) <u>So also, *is* the resurrection of the dead. It is sown in corruption; it is raised in incorruption:</u>

(43) <u>It is sown in dishonor; it is raised in glory: it is sown in weakness; it is raised in power:</u>

(**44**) It is sown a natural body; it is raised a spiritual body. There is a natural body, and there is a spiritual body.

(**45**) And so it is written, the first man Adam was made a living soul; the last Adam *was made* a quickening spirit.

(**46**) Howbeit that *was* not first which is spiritual, but that which is natural; and afterward that which is spiritual.

(**47**) The first man *is* of the earth, earthy: the second man *is* the Lord from heaven.

(**48**) As *is* the earthy, such *are* they also that are earthy: and as *is* the heavenly, such *are* they also that are heavenly.

(**49**) And as we have borne the image of the earthy, we shall also bear the image of the heavenly.

(**50**) Now this I say, brethren, that flesh and blood cannot inherit the kingdom of God; neither doth corruption inherit incorruption.

(**51**) Behold, I shew you a mystery; We shall not all sleep, but we shall all be changed,

So, according to Paul's writings, we have two bodies, a spiritual body, and a natural body or as I teach, a flesh body. When or how did this take place; that is, how did we wound up with two bodies, one inside the other?

To find our answer, we'll have to go back to the very beginning. OK, let's go to the beginning; we see in the first book of the bible, 'It says, In the beginning, God created the Heaven and the Earth... No, that's not what I'm talking about; I mean the very beginning of everything. Genesis is only, for the most part, talking about the start of this physical or flesh creation. I mean the very beginning of everything.

In the gospel of John, we read the words, 'In the beginning was the word, and the word was with God and the word was God. (John 1:1)

English ------------------Greek

Word ------------------- Logo

'Logo' in the Greek language means more than just the written word; it also means 'spoke person'.

So, in my mind the above verse from John could have been written, 'In the beginning was a spoke person and the spoke person was with God and the spoke person was God'.

John 1:1-14

(1) In the beginning was the Word, and the Word was with God, and the Word was God.

(2) The same was in the beginning with God.

(3) All things were made by him; and without him was not anything made that was made.

(4) In him was life; and the life was the light of men.

(5) And the light shines in darkness; and the darkness comprehended it not.

(6) There was a man sent from God, whose name was John.

(7) The same came for a witness, to bear witness of the light, that all men through him might believe.

(8) He was not that light but was sent to bear witness of that light.

(9) That was the true light, which lights every man that comes into the world.

(10) He was in the world, and the world was made by him, and the world knew him not.

(11) He came unto his own, and his own received him not.

(12) But as many as received him, to them gave he power to become the sons of God, even to them who believe on his name:

(13) Which were born, not of blood, nor of the will of the flesh, nor of the will of man, but of God.

(14) And the Word was made flesh, and dwelt among us, (and we beheld his glory, the glory as of

the only begotten of the Father,) full of grace and truth.

This is how it started, God, our Creator, Heavenly Father, or whatever name you use to visualize your maker was by himself and didn't like what he saw in a vast void. So, what did he do about it? We read in the book of Revelation that God created all things for his pleasure, or as it reads, 'Thou are worthy, O Lord, to receive glory and honor and power: for thou have created all things, and for thy pleasure they are created'. (Revelation 4:11)

Have you given God pleasure in your life? I hope so; most of us haven't.

Ok, what happens next? What was the most important thing on Gods mind? Since we are created in God's image, what is the most important thing on our minds? I mean after we have gotten all the materials things we desire. I ask this because God has all things of a material nature he could every want and if there is something he wants and doesn't have, he has the power to create it. Agree? What would you want if you had all things? Would it be someone to share your good fortunate and life with? Family; children? That's right, all the treasures of the world are nothing if you don't have someone to share it with. So, I believe God felt the same way and what did he do? He created his Children; how many? I don't know but based on the population of the Earth at present and the number of people who have died in the past; I would guess the number of sons he created would be around 20 billion; maybe more. Remember, I'm just guessing.

Perhaps you are wondering how I can state, God created his sons first? It's in the bible. Christ told us in the gospel of Mark that he has foretold us all things. (Mark 13:23) So where did God tell us he created his sons first? We find our answer in the book of Job. (Job 38:4-7)

(4) Where was thou when I laid the foundations of the earth? Declare if thou have understanding.

(5) Who has laid the measures thereof if thou know? Or who has stretched the line upon it?

(6) Whereupon are the foundations thereof fastened? Or who laid the corner stone thereof.

(7) When the morning stars sang together, and all the sons of God shouted for joy?

Did you see it? The sons of God, the stars, couldn't have shouted for joy unless they had already been created. So, they were created first.

Now this next part is what I believe, and I don't have a lot of scripture to back up what I'm about to put on paper.

When God created his children, they were not all created equal; that is, they didn't all have the same abilities. They were created to do the job or work God needed or wanted them to do. Now we have a universe full of God's children doing the work assigned to each individual and everything is perfect, just the way God wanted it; Right?

Well, almost; there is one small hiccup to be dealt with. Did I say small? Of course, I'm talking about Lucifer; the Archangel whom God created to be one of the Cherub to protect the mercy seat of God. Did you know Lucifer was created to be a protector of

God's Kingdom? But what happened; instead of protecting the mercy seat of God, Lucifer wanted to sit on this mercy seat. He wanted to be the ruler of God's children instead of God. He felt he was more qualified. Or as it states below in this excerpt from the book of Ezekiel.

(Ezekiel 28:12-15)

(**12**) Son of man, take up a lamentation upon the king of Tyrus, and say unto him, Thus saith the Lord GOD; Thou sealest up the sum, full of wisdom, and perfect in beauty.

(**13**) Thou hast been in Eden the garden of God; every precious stone *was* thy covering, the sardius, topaz, and the diamond, the beryl, the onyx, and the jasper, the sapphire, the emerald, and the carbuncle, and gold: the workmanship of thy tabrets and of thy pipes was prepared in thee in the day that thou was created.

(**14**) Thou *art* the anointed cherub that covered; and I have set thee *so*: thou was upon the holy mountain of God; thou hast walked up and down in the midst of the stones of fire.

(**15**) <u>Thou *was* perfect in thy ways from the day</u> <u>that thou were created, till iniquity was found in thee.</u>

From reading the above scriptures, we can conclude, Lucifer started out being good and doing good; but his nature changed. How could this be you're wondering? Didn't God create something good? How can it turn evil and become a sinner? Like you and me, God gave his creation free choice or free will, if you choose to think that way. This is the same as he has given us; to love him or not love him; our choice and also Lucifer's choice.

Lucifer chose not to love God and also, he wanted to replace God. He believed he was more powerful than God. He still does today; well, maybe not more powerful than God, but smarter than God would be a better way of putting it. What did he do? Our answer is given in the book of Revelation in chapter 12. (Rev 12:3-10)

(**3**) <u>And there appeared another wonder in</u> <u>heaven; and behold a great red dragon, having seven</u> <u>heads and ten horns, and seven crowns upon his</u> <u>heads.</u>

(4) And his tail drew the third part of the stars of heaven, and did cast them to the earth: and the dragon stood before the woman which was ready to be delivered, for to devour her child as soon as it was born.

(5) And she brought forth a man child, who was to rule all nations with a rod of iron: and her child was caught up unto God, and *to* his throne.

(6) And the woman fled into the wilderness, where she hath a place prepared of God, that they should feed her there a thousand two hundred *and* threescore days.

(7) And there was war in heaven: Michael and his angels fought against the dragon; and the dragon fought and his angels,

(8) And prevailed not; neither was their place found any more in heaven.

(9) And the great dragon was cast out, that old serpent, called the Devil, and Satan, which deceived the whole world: he was cast out into the earth, and his angels were cast out with him.

(**10**) <u>And I heard a loud voice saying in heaven, Now is come salvation, and strength, and the kingdom of our God, and the power of his Christ: for the accuser of our brethren is cast down, which accused them before our God day and night.</u>

Lucifer's plan at becoming the Supreme Ruler of the universe was put down and he along with his followers were cast out of Heaven unto the earth where they have remained even unto today.

OK, where are they, you might ask? I'll tell in just a little bit, but first, I want to let you read how our heavenly Father felt because of this rebellion from his children. This insert is from the book of Jeremiah. Remember the rebellion has been put down and God is looking at the destruction his rebellious children have brought in their act of war.

In the next paragraph is our Father's thoughts after he has destroyed everything and put down the rebellion.

Jeremiah 4:23-27)

(23) <u>I beheld the earth, and, lo, *it was* without form, and void; and the heavens, and they *had* no light.</u>

(24) <u>I beheld the mountains, and, lo, they trembled, and all the hills moved lightly.</u>

(25) <u>I beheld, and, lo, *there was* no man, and all the birds of the heavens were fled.</u>

(26) <u>I beheld, and, lo, the fruitful place *was* a wilderness, and all the cities thereof were broken down at the presence of the LORD, *and* by his fierce anger.</u>

(27) <u>For thus hath the LORD said, the whole land shall be desolate; yet will I not make a full end.</u>

Again, we are looking at a bad translation from the Hebrew into English. The English word 'was' is not in the manuscripts. It is a word added to the scripture to make the reading easier to understand the regeneration of the planet Earth.

The verse should read; 'I beheld the earth, and, lo, it became without form, and void; and the heavens, and they had no light.' Who or what is the 'light'? Christ is the light; God removed him from the

1st earth age when he destroyed everything. The light is the savior of God's handiwork and without the light, nothing lives. Perhaps, now you will understand why the world went dark when our Christ was killed on the Roman cross. But praise be to God, when Christ was resurrected back to life, the world was not left in darkness.

Now, we can begin our study of genesis.

Genesis 1:1

(1) In the beginning, God created the heaven and the earth.

(2) And the earth was (became) without form, and void; and darkness was (became) upon the face of the deep. And the spirit of God moved upon the face of the waters.

I think we need to take a second look at this sentence. The word 'was' is not in the manuscripts and most King James Versions of the bible have this word in italics. Why, might you ask? My answer is the Hebrew word translated 'was' is 'hayah' and would be better translated as 'became'; because the Hebrew word, Hayah, is a form or the verb to be or become.

Likewise, the same of the Hebrew word, 'mayin', it does not translate to waters directly. Like a lot of English words, it translates by how it is used in a sentence; but can we be sure of God's message is being given by using waters as the correct translation?

'Mayin' translates as "dual of a prim. Noun (but used in a sing. Sense); water: fig. juice; by euphem. Urine, semen + piss, wasting, water (ing, course, flood, spring). So, you see the Hebrew use for this word, Mayin, is more in dealing with people than rivers or oceans.

(3) And God said, let there be light: and there was light.

(4) And God saw the light, that it was good: and God divided the light from the darkness.

We know Christ is the light, so who is the darkness? Lucifer and his followers; except now we need not call him Lucifer anymore because he is no longer the 'morning star'. Now we will call him 'Satan', meaning adversary, because he is against everything Christ will do.

(5) And God called the light Day, and the darkness he called Night. And the evening and the morning were the first day.

Notice the bible has the words 'Day' and 'Night' capitalized. Why? My thinking, the Hebrew word translated Day is 'yown' and literally means 'hot' and a whole lot of other things. I think God is trying to show his followers are completely opposite of Satan's followers. I say this because the Hebrew word translated 'Night' is 'lavil' and among other things it can translate to is 'adversity'. The difference between Night and Day is the same as the difference between Christ and Satan.

In verse five, we see the new day starts at sundown when it is getting dark. Most everyone will agree bad things happen at night in the darkness than in the light or daytime. Also, we know from reading God's word that Satan comes at the six trump and Christ doesn't come back to the earth until the seventh trump. Maybe, this is one of the ways God is telling us how it will be in the end times.

(6) And God said, let there be a firmament in the mist of the waters, and let it divide the waters from the waters.

(7) And God made the firmament and divided the waters which were under the firmament from the waters which were above the firmament: and it was so.

(8) And God called the firmament Heaven. And the evening and morning were the second day.

If you consider the 'waters' as just being liquid, verses 6, 7, and 8 doesn't make much sense, but if you look at the waters as being people, you have a whole new scenario.

In the book of Revelation, chapter 17:15, we read,

(15) And he said unto me, the waters which thou saw, where the whore sits, are peoples, and multitudes, and nations, and tongues.

In this verse from the book of Revelation, God tells us the waters are peoples, and etc. Would this also hold for the book of Genesis? It would make more sense to me if this were the case; it would follow in my mind to separate the good from the bad, especially after the revolt Satan caused in God's kingdom; what do you think?

Continuing in the book of Genesis, verse 9.

(9) And God said, let the waters under the heaven be gather together in one place, and let the dry land appear: and it was so.

(10) And God called the dry land Earth; and the gathering together of the waters called the seas, and God saw that it was good.

Simply explanation, right? Yes, except for one thing, the Hebrew manuscripts do not include the word 'land'; it was added by the translators. Why? I don't know except they might have not realized what the word translated 'dry' really meant.

So, the Hebrew word translated dry is 'yabbashah' and it means dry alright, but dry what? Researching further into the origin of this word, 'yabbashah' and we find it is derived from the Hebrew word 'yabesh' which translates as disappointed; to be ashamed; confused. Are you waking up now? God is not talking about any dry land, but his sons who went astray and followed Satan in his rebellion against the Father.

I believe a better translation of the verses 9 and 10 in the book of Genesis would be: "And God said, let the rebellious children left on earth and under heaven be gather together in one place and let the ashamed ones appear. And God called the ashamed ones, Earth, (meaning, the ones who didn't stand against Satan's rebellion or help Michael and his followers stand with God; theses would be left on earth along with Satan followers) and the gathering together of the people called the masses of people, and God saw that it was good."

My thinking, perhaps you disagree? If so, that's alright with me; your choice. Continuing on.

(11) And God said, let the earth bring forth grass, the herb yielding seed, and the fruit tree yielding fruit after his kind, whose seed is in itself, upon the earth; and it was so.

(12) And the earth brought forth grass. And herb yielding seed after his kind, and the tree yielding

fruit, whose seed was in itself, after his kind: and God saw that it was good.

(13) And the evening and the morning were the third day.

This all looks good at first glance, but what or who is being described here? I think, because of the discussion so far, God is still talking about his children. Could it be that the grass, the herb, the tree are different breeds of people God planted on earth? My thinking, the scripture gives us this image that a tree will have fruit after 'his' kind, not after 'it's' kind. The scripture uses personal pronouns for the description of what is to take place. Why? We have only three original races of breeds on earth; the Negro or black skinned man, the White skinned man, and the yellow skinned man or Orientals. This is how the races started and we all come from one or the other or a mix of these races.

I believe starting with verse 14 of the book of Genesis, the translators got it about right. Now God is dealing with the physical life and what it takes to sustain this type of life on the newly construed planet earth. Notice, God creates physical man and woman in his image; I don't know if he places a spirit of one of his children in these newly formed humans or not. The bible doesn't say at this point. Anyway, the first six days are up or maybe it is 6000 years. As we read in the book of 2 Peter, 3:8,

2 Peter 3:8

But, beloved, be not ignorant of this one thing, that one day is with the Lord as a thousand years, and a thousand years as one day.

Chapter 2

Alright, we have finished with the earth being made habitable for flesh life to live on the planet. When God finished his work on preparing the planet for physical life, he took a break and surveyed his work and he liked what he saw, or as the bible puts it.

Genesis 2:1-3

(1) Thus, the heavens, and the earth were finished, and all the host of them.

(2) And on the seventh day God ended his work which he had made; and he rested on the seventh day from all his work which he had made.

(3) And God blessed the seventh day and sanctified it; because that in it he had rested from all his work which God created and made.

The rejuvenation of the earth is completed, and flesh mankind, male and female are complete. What happens next?

If you reread verse 26 in the first chapter of Genesis, you'll notice when he created the first men and women, they were created to be hunters and fishermen.

Genesis 1:27 & 28

(27) So, God created man in his own image, in the image of God created he him; male and female created he them.

(28) And God blessed them, and God said unto them, be fruitful, and multiply, and replenish the earth, and subdue it; and have dominion over the fish of the sea, and over the fowl of the air, and over every living thing that moves upon the earth.

What's lacking in God's creation? He doesn't have a farmer or a husbandman. What is God going to do to correct or add to his creation; he going to create a man for the task and place him in a 'garden' to see how he will react. The bible tells us God planted a garden eastward in Eden and put the man he created in it.

Genesis 2:7-9

Now let us enter into the "Garden of Eden" and see what's taking place there. It is now the eighth day of God's rejuvenation of the earth. Remember, he created the races on the sixth day and rested on the seventh; so now it is the eighth day, and we are about to see Adam being created. From the bible, we read, "And the Lord God formed man of the dust of the ground and breathed into his nostrils the breath of life; and man became a living soul. And the Lord God planted a garden eastward in Eden; and there he put the man whom he had formed. And out of the ground made the Lord God to grow every tree that is pleasant to the sight, and good for food' the tree of life also in the midst of the garden, and the tree of knowledge of good and evil." (Genesis 2:7-9) Adam becoming a living soul is a little bit misleading. The Hebrew word translated "soul" is "nephesh" and properly translated would say Adam became a living creature or animal. Adam didn't have a spirit of one of God's children placed in him because he was created by God. To have a spirit placed in his body would show Christ to be a liar. We learned earlier in our discussion of Christ and Nicodemus about when a spirit is placed into a human body. Christ, as stated before, answered, "Verily, verily, I say unto thee, except a man be born of water and of the Spirit, he cannot enter into the kingdom of God." (John 3:5) Meaning the children of God all have to enter this world by being born of woman. The mention of water is referring to a baby being born when the woman's water breaks. Without this birth through woman, God states they will not ascend back to heaven. Further, Christ reminds Nicodemus that even the natural Son of God has to follow the same rules when he stated, "And no man hath ascended up to heaven, but he that came down from heaven, even the Son of man which is in heaven. (John 3:13)

So, Adam had the life force as all animals. Like dogs and cats, and etc.; but no spirit from the 1st earth age was placed in him or Eve. The only ones who would have a spirit placed in them would be their children.

So, does this mean Adam would never ascend to Heaven at his death? No, try to visualize the 'Garden of Eden' being already in Heaven and Adam with a spiritual body. He was not created to ever die; neither was Eve. They were created to give birth to all the sinful children God changed into spirits. Nobody was ever supposed to experience 'death'. The children Eve would bring into this world would live and learn God's way of living and enter into a loving relationship with their Father. When God breathe the breath of life into Adam, he became a living soul; not a mortal man, but when he sinned, his righteous body changed, and he was condemned to death and all his descendants were now under the penalty of death of the spirit.

Because of their sin, Adam and Eve were expelled from the 'Garden of Eden' and sent to live in a physical world with pain and sweat and suffering. The bible tells us Cherubims and a flaming sword which turned every way, to keep the way of the tree of life. I interpreted this last sentence to mean God at this time separated the spiritual world where God lives from the physical world by a veil where each side cannot see into the other realm unless God wants to raise the veil for his purpose to be carried out. (See; 2 Kings 6:17) We could call this a different dimension if it helps you understand what I'm writing easier.

Now, I know you are worried about Adam and Eve not being able to ascend to Heaven because they weren't born of women; but Christ said they couldn't ascend unless they came from Heaven. Right! But they did come from Heaven; that's where they were before God kicked them out and made them physical. They are in Heaven now; I don't know which side of the 'gulf' they are in, but they are there.

After God created Adam, he formed or created all the domestic animal's man would need in his work as a farmer. After they were formed of the dust of the ground, God brought them before Adam, and he gave each one of them a name. (Genesis 2:19-20) After this project is completed, God decides to go ahead and make Adam a helper or helpmate. God already knew how lonely Adam was without someone to share his daily life. (Genesis 2:18) God could have brought a woman to Adam from the races he had created on the sixth day; but God wanted a pure line from Adam to Christ. What I'm saying is, God created Adam as a special case for his Son to be born from this bloodline, a pure undefiled pedigree from Adam to Christ. How was God to accomplish this?

The bible informs us God caused a deep sleep to fall on Adam and while unconscious, he removed a rib and made a woman. (Genesis 2:21-22) The actual written word from the bible states: "And the Lord God caused a deep sleep to fall upon Adam, and he slept: and he took one of his ribs and closed up the flesh instead thereof; And the rib, which the Lord God had taken from man, made he a woman, and bought her unto the man."

I've heard preachers say man has one less rib in their bodies than women because of this act of God. Of course, this is not true; men and women have the same number of ribs. Contrary to popular thought, this isn't what the Hebrew manuscripts say at all. The word "rib" is a mistranslation; the correct word is "curve". The manuscripts read that God took a curve from Adam and used this curve to create the woman, Eve. The only curve the 1611 translators could visualize in a person's body was the rib. The technology of that time period in history had not discovered the Helices Curve or the DNA of every person's physical body. We know about the DNA of the body today; therefore, we can understand, God was talking about removing a part of the DNA curve from Adam. God removed the basic female portions of the DNA curve from man and used it to make a woman. Have you ever wondered why a woman thinks different from a man? Her mental make-up is different; even her hearing centers are different. A woman has two hearing centers in her brain; she can talk and listen at the same time. Man can't do this; he either talks or listens.

Have you ever wondered why a man and a woman are so attracted to each other, besides the obvious sexual desire? IT TAKES BOTH TO MAKE A COMPLETE UNIT!

So now, we have a newly created man and woman in the Garden of Eden. What next? They had to be schooled; educated as to what the new rebirth earth had in store for them. This is what the "trees" in the garden was all about. The trees weren't fruit or nut bearing plants; but instructors of God, angels if you will understand. The clue is right before your eyes in that the tree of life is in the midst of the garden (Christ) and the tree of knowledge of good and evil represent Satan. So, why would you even consider any of the other trees to be anything besides instructors, even though they are called trees as Christ was called the Tree of Life.

As stated, "And all the trees of the field shall know that I the Lord have brought down the high tree, have exalted the low tree, have dried up the green tree, and have made the dry tree to flourish, I the Lord have spoken and have done it." (Ezekiel 17:24) here God is describing the Pharez line and the Zerah line in the tribe of Judah. The Pharez line is the bloodline Christ was born through; the Zerah line was cast out and left the country; finally settling in Ireland. We'll talk about the Zerah line settling in Ireland in another discussion. Also, as stated in Ezekiel, "The cedars in the garden of God could not hide him: the fir trees were not like his boughs, and the chestnut trees were not like his branches; nor any tree in the garden of God was like unto him in his beauty. I have made him fair by the multitude of his branches: so that all the trees of Eden, that were in the garden of God envied him." (Ezekiel 31:8 & 9) Don't let the trees confuse your thinking in this lesson.

Just let this sink in and keep your mind tuned to the trees in God's word being people and not plants. Read the whole chapter 31 of Ezekiel where God is comparing Pharaoh to the arch-angel Satan; and showing how Satan was brought to nothing by God, and how Pharaoh will be done the same.

The Hebrew word translated "ground" is "adamah" and has a lot of meanings. They are country, earth, ground, husband, and land; the better translation would be "husband", meaning from our God, the Father. Since he is the creator, he is also the Father of all his children or a husband. If this "flew over your head", put it on a back burner and let it simmer for a while; someday it will make sense to you.

Why did God put Satan in the garden? The bible doesn't really say; but my guess would be, God wanted to see how he would behave since the rebellion has been put down and Satan had been demoted in rank. He may have wanted to test his new creation; that is, Adam and Eve. So, what happened? Satan didn't waste any time in conning Eve into disobeying God. Eve tried to use God's statements to keep Satan at arm's length by quoting what God told Adam, "ye shall not eat of it, neither shall ye touch it, lest ye die." This word touch doesn't convey much though if you're talking about a tree; but if you are talking about a person, there's a whole new scenario opened up. In this case, God was talking about a person; he was referring to Satan. He was warning Adam not to have anything to do with Satan, either from his teachings or in a sexual capacity. (Genesis 3:3) And what else would happen if Adam disobeyed God? God said "lest ye die"; what did God mean by this statement? We learn from Paul's teaching in Romans, the wages of sin are death (Rom. 3:23) So I think we can deduct from God's command and from Paul's teaching concerning Adam and Eve along with Satan's seduction, the perfect man and woman God planned to use to bring his many wayward children back to him has hit a snag. Now, all mankind has come under a death sentence. All children born into this world carry the death penalty of their spirit and cannot enter into Heaven where the Father and Christ reside. They are now condemned to wait on the wrong side of the gulf which separates Christ and his followers from Satan's followers and the ones who never knew who Christ was. This is what the parable

Christ gave about the Rich man and Lazarus is really about. Christ showed there are two parts to Heaven. One where the ones who haven't accepted Christ as Lord reside until the millennium arrives and is separated by a wide 'gulf' from the place in Heaven where Christ and his followers live. In the bible this place is called the grave. The bible is not very clear in what this means at this point, but we do know Adam and Eve were cast out of the 'Garden of Eden' and their bodies were changed from a spiritual body to a flesh body because of their sins.

We all know what happened; Eve liked what she saw and wanted to be wise in the ways of the world, so she accepted the seduction of Satan and had sex with him. Later, she brought Adam to Satan and he did "eat". (Genesis 3:6) My guess is that they had a three-way sexual orgy, and their "eyes" were opened. (Genesis 3:7) They were no more the innocent children God created but grown adults in a world of life and death, sin, and sorrow. The bible informs us that they sewed fig leaves together to make aprons because they knew they were naked. (Genesis 3:7)

Have you ever tried to sew green leaves together? It doesn't work and besides where did they get the needle and thread. There wasn't any around at this time. The correct translation from the Hebrew manuscripts say they made a poultice from the fruit of the fig and pasted the mixture over their private parts or the part of the human body where the sin was committed.

Was God happy with his children? Their actions brought God down to see for himself what was taking place on earth. (Genesis 3:8) He asked Adam about being "naked" and "eating of the tree". What did Adam do? Did he confess his sin to God and ask for forgiveness? No! He placed all the blame on Eve. (Genesis 3:12)

So, God catches up with Eve and ask her basically the same question. What did she say? She answered right! She said the Serpent beguiled me and I committed the sin. Most theologians teach the word "beguiled" to mean Eve was tricked by the serpent into believing God had lied to her; but the manuscripts give the word to mean "wholly seduced".

In the New Testament, Paul treats the subject as Eve being "wholly seduced" in his letter to the Corinthians (2 Cor. 11:3) Here the word "beguiled" is translated from the Greek word "exapatao". What happens when a woman is seduced by a man? She has sex with him!

Next, God speaks to the serpent (Satan). There are no questions asked; only a judgment concerning the events which had taken place because the evil one knew what he was doing. Satan has a curse placed on him in the form of further demoting in rank or responsibilities. (Genesis 3:14) He's no longer in charge of anything in God's kingdom; he is an outcast. No wonder Isaiah was inspired to write, "How art thou fallen from heaven, O Lucifer, son of the morning! How art thou cut down to the ground, which didst weaken the Nations!" (Isa. 14:12)

But God doesn't stop with this demoting. God tells Satan what will happen in the future if there is no change in his attitude. God tells him, "I will put enmity between thee and the woman, and between thy seed and her seed; it shall bruise thy head, and thou shall bruise his heel." (Genesis 3:15)

The English word "seed" is translated from the Hebrew word "Zera" which has a lot of meanings. (fruit, plant, posterity, carnally, child, etc.) In the New Testament and speaking on the same subject, the Greek word is "sperma" of which the English word "sperm" or male sperm is derived.

This is the first prophesy of Christ in the bible; because of the mess Satan contributed to in the "Garden of Eden", the world will now need a savior to reconcile all of God's children back to God. There will have to be a blood sacrifice to wash away the sins of the world. (Hebrews 9:22) God, himself, made this sacrifice through Jesus Christ and his death on the cross.

Next, God speaks to Eve again and tells her she is pregnant from this three-way sexual encounter with Adam and Satan. (Genesis 3:16) She will have twin sons; one will be Adam's child and one will be Satan's child.

Satan's son, "Cain", will come first; this is symbolic of the end times when Satan will come first claiming to be the Christ. After Cain is born, Eve continues in labor and brings forth another child who is named Abel. (And again, she bares his brother Abel; this word "again" is from the Hebrew word "yacaph" and means "to continue"; as in Eve's case, it means to continue in labor until Abel was born. - Genesis 4:2) Abel is the true son of Adam and depicts the true Son of God entering the world after Satan. We are approaching the end of time, and God is watching to see who has done their homework; and who knows not to worship the false Christ when he arrives on the world scene. Some Christians will think the rapture is taking place and will be waiting to fly away with Satan because they will believe he is the Christ. REMEMBER, Satan comes first to set up his one world government; don't be deceived into worshipping him as the Christ.

When the two boys, Cain, and Abel, reached the age of accountability, they make a sacrifice or offering to the Lord. Abel brought the best he had, and his offering was accepted by the Lord; but Cain brought in second best and gave it to the Lord and God rejected his offering. (Genesis 4:3-5) In the next verse, we see God speaking to Cain as if he were an unwanted stepchild. He is told by God to pick his head up and try; if he does well, he'll be accepted and if he doesn't, it will be because of sin in his life, not because of his birth or heritage. (Genesis 4:6-7) This is an important promise to the sons of Cain; that is, the Kenites. Even though they are the children of Satan (Serpent), God will judge them the same as the rest of his children. They will be judged by their faith and their works. Most won't respond to God's drawing of the Holy Spirit; but hopefully some will come to know the love of God.

We know Cain killed his brother Abel and chose the way of the world; the way his father Satan does business. For his punishment, God drove Cain away from Adam and Eve and he settled in the land of Nod (Genesis 4:17&17) and took a wife there of the sixth day of rejuvenation of the earth. (Genesis 1:24 thru 31)

So, there you have it; the story of the true facts concerning the "Garden of Eden". Or do you really understand the meaning of the story; it's more than just two children going astray. This story takes place in the life of all children born of woman. We call it the age of accountability and it's a different physical age among God's children. Some are nine or ten years of age and others are fifty or sixty years of age; the age when you wake up and realize there's more to this physical life span than you had ever considered is the age of accountability. It's the age when you finally realize God exists and you have a choice to make; follow God or follow the ways of the world. Christ said, "I came that you might have life and to have it more abundantly". (John 10:10) Will you wake up and accept God's way of life through his Son, Jesus, and work in the kingdom to bring more sons and daughters into the kingdom of God. God loves you and wants you with him for all eternity; but if you refuse, his promise is that he will blot you out in the "lake of Fire".

Chapter 3

Has Satan been successful in averting God's plan to save a third of his children who followed Lucifer and rebelled against our Creator? What about the ones who didn't back either side? This kind of reminds me of the people living today.

We know Satan didn't win; Satan's small win in the 'Garden of Eden' only causes more pain for God's children who now have to go through their physical life in the flesh body. Because of the sin committed by Adam, his family is ejected from the beautiful 'Garden' God built for him. Now he'll have to provide for himself and his family by toil and working the land by the sweat of his brow.

For those of you who may not know what God considers 'Sin', the answer is given in the book of 1 John 3:4 and it reads:

1 John 3:4

Whosoever commits sin also transgresses the law: for sin is the transgression of the law.

What is law? Law is breaking a commandant of God. At the time of the 'Garden of Eden', God had only given one law. God said, "ye shall not eat of it, neither shall ye touch it, lest ye die." This is the first commandment or law given by God. At this time no other law or laws have been given by our Creator. This could be why God was lenient to Cain when he murdered Abel; no law against murder had been given by God.

Cain goes into the land of Nod and takes a wife; this further proof the races were all created before Adam and Eve came on the scene. By this time in our history, the world has become populated with people. We also see the descendants of Adam and Eve multiply greatly; some living almost a thousand years. Other than long life, not much is happening. It is recorded in Chapter 5 of Genesis, beginning with verse one.

(1) This is the book of the generations of Adam. In the day that God created man, in the likeness of God made he him.

(2) Male and female created he them; and blessed them, and called their name Adam, in the day when they were created.

(3) And Adam lived a hundred and thirty years, and begat a son in his own likeness, after his image; and called his name Seth:

(4) And the days of Adam after he had begotten Seth were eight hundred years: and he begat sons and daughters:

(5) And all the days that Adam lived were nine hundred and thirty years: and he died.

(6) And Seth lived a hundred and five years, and begat Enos:

(7) And Seth lived after he begat Enos eight hundred and seven years, and begat sons and daughters:

(8) And all the days of Seth were nine hundred and twelve years: and he died.

(9) And Enos lived ninety years, and begat Cainan:

(10) And Enos lived after he begat Cainan eight hundred and fifteen years, and begat sons and daughters:

(11) And all the days of Enos were nine hundred and five years: and he died.

(12) And Cainan lived seventy years, and begat Mahalaleel:

(13) And Cainan lived after he begat Mahalaleel eight hundred and forty years, and begat sons and daughters:

(14) And all the days of Cainan were nine hundred and ten years: and he died.

(15) And Mahalaleel lived sixty and five years, and begat Jared:

(16) And Mahalaleel lived after he begat Jared eight hundred and thirty years, and begat sons and daughters:

(17) And all the days of Mahalaleel were eight hundred ninety and five years: and he died.

(18) And Jared lived a hundred sixty and two years, and he begat Enoch:

(19) And Jared lived after he begat Enoch eight hundred years, and begat sons and daughters:

(20) And all the days of Jared were nine hundred sixty and two years: and he died.

21And Enoch lived sixty and five years, and begat Methuselah:

(22) And Enoch walked with God after he begat Methuselah three hundred years, and begat sons and daughters:

(23) And all the days of Enoch were three hundred sixty and five years:

(24) And Enoch walked with God: and he was not; for God took him.

(25) And Methuselah lived a hundred eighty and seven years, and begat Lamech:

(26) And Methuselah lived after he begat Lamech seven hundred eighty and two years, and begat sons and daughters:

(27) And all the days of Methuselah were nine hundred sixty and nine years: and he died.

(28) And Lamech lived a hundred eighty and two years, and begat a son:

(29) And he called his name Noah, saying, this same shall comfort us concerning our work and toil of our hands, because of the ground which the LORD hath cursed.

(30) And Lamech lived after he begat Noah five hundred ninety and five years, and begat sons and daughters:

(31) And all the days of Lamech were seven hundred seventy and seven years: and he died.

(32) And Noah was five hundred years old: and Noah begat Shem, Ham, and Japheth.

I gave you this list of Adam's descendants so you can readily see how the earth became heavily populated by Noah time on earth.

Of all these offspring from Adam, only Enoch does the right thing in God's eyes and what happens? Enoch doesn't die in the physical body; he is translated and sent back to Heaven to be with our Father. See verse 24.

All these years, God has given only one command; don't have anything to do with Satan. period.

There's not much said about Satan and what he is doing at this time in history, but we are told Angels start coming to earth and began mating with the daughters of men.

Genesis 6:1

(1) And it came to pass, when men began to multiply on the face of the earth, and daughters were born unto them,

(2) That the sons of God saw the daughters of men that they were fair; and they took them wives of all which they chose.

The bible doesn't tell us, but I suspect Satan was behind this effort to pollute all the flesh people on earth. He knows God's plan to bring a savior, Christ, into the physical world through a purebred descendant of Adam and Eve. I believe Satan figured if he could stop the savior from every being born into this flesh world in a human body descended from Adam and Eve, none of God's wayward children could be forgiven of their sin debt and thereby keep God from destroying him in the lake of fire, because God had already shown he cared more for his children than he did for the entire universe of suns and planets by destroying everything except his children. If he killed Satan, he would have to kill all the ones who followed Satan in the revolt. God is fair, Satan knows this and tries to use God's nature against him in his effort to stay his sentence from being carried out. So, what is God going to do to stop Satan and the fallen Angels efforts to thwart justice? This God's answer to the problem.

Genesis 6:4-7

(4) There were giants in the earth in those days; and also, after that, when the sons of God came in unto the daughters of men, and they birth children

to them, the same became mighty men which were of old, men of renown.

(5) And GOD saw that the wickedness of man was great in the earth, and that every imagination of the thoughts of his heart was only evil continually.

(6) And it repented the LORD that he had made man on the earth, and it grieved him at his heart.

(7) And the LORD said, I will destroy man whom I have created from the face of the earth; both man, and beast, and the creeping thing, and the fowls of the air; for it repents me that I have made them.

Now, God decides mankind is so wicked, there is no reason to keep his plan in tack; he decides to destroy all flesh on earth which breaths air to survive. But in scanning all humanity, he sees one family who hasn't mixed with the fallen Angels and still has a pure descend from Adam in tack. This is Noah and his children.

Genesis 6:8

(8) But Noah found grace in the eyes of the LORD.

(9) 9These are the generations of Noah: Noah was a just man and perfect in his generations, and Noah walked with God.

(10) And Noah begat three sons, Shem, Ham, and Japheth.

(11) The earth also was corrupt before God, and the earth was filled with violence.

(12) And God looked upon the earth, and behold, it was corrupt; for all flesh had corrupted his way upon the earth.

(13) And God said unto Noah, the end of all flesh is come before me; for the earth is filled with violence through them; and behold I will destroy them with the earth.

I want to point out here for the ones who might think Noah was without sin; God only said he was a just man and had a perfect pedigree all the way back to Adam.

Why was the earth corrupt and filled with violence; why had all flesh corrupted his way upon the earth? Just my thinking; there were no rules to live by; no form of government in all the land. At this time

God had given only one law: never have anything to do with Satan, period. But where is Satan at this time? The scriptures don't mention his name; but where did God condemn him to live? On the Earth!

Genesis 3:14 tells us:

(14) And the LORD God said unto the serpent because thou hast done this, thou art cursed above all cattle, and above every beast of the field; upon thy belly shalt thou go, and dust shalt thou eat all the days of thy life.

Where will we find dust for the Serpent to eat? On the earth; as it says in the first chapter of Genesis, God left all his wayward children under the firmament of Heaven. Again, when we look in the book of Job, what do we read?

Job 1:6 &7

(6) Now there was a day when the sons of God came to present themselves before the LORD, and Satan came also among them.

(7) And the LORD said unto Satan, Whence comest thou? Then Satan answered the LORD, and

said, from going to and fro in the earth, and from walking up and down in it.

So, we should understand, Satan has been imprisoned on earth since the 'Garden of Eden'. When Satan tempted Christ where did this take place? You did say 'in the wilderness', didn't you? That's right; on this earth!

Matthew 4:1

Then was Jesus led up of the Spirit into the wilderness to be tempted of the devil.

That's right; on this earth!

What is God going to do about the corruption on earth? My thinking: he's going to destroy the corruption on earth along with the ones who caused it. But here, the scriptures get a bit tricky. According to the King James Bible, Noah and his children plus their wives are the only ones God saves from the flood of the earth God is about to bring about. That's eight people plus all the animals God will bring on board the Ark.

It takes Noah and his children 120 years to build the Ark and from the dimensions given in the bible, I picture the Ark looking like a long hollowed out 2x4 with a window in the top of the Ark. When it is finished, the Ark measures 450 ft long by 75 ft wide and 45 ft tall and all the ones God wants in the Ark are placed in their respected places, God shuts the door to the Ark and the rains began.

Genesis 6:14-22

(14) Make thee an ark of gopher wood; rooms shalt thou make in the ark, and shalt pitch it within and without with pitch.

(15) And this is the fashion which thou shalt make it of: The length of the ark shall be three hundred cubits, the breadth of it fifty cubits, and the height of it thirty cubits.

(16) A window shalt thou make to the ark, and in a cubit shalt thou finish it above; and the door of the ark shalt thou set in the side thereof; with lower, second, and third stories shalt thou make it.

(17) And behold, I, even I, do bring a flood of waters upon the earth, to destroy all flesh, wherein is the breath of life, from under heaven; and everything that is in the earth shall die.

(18) But with thee will I establish my covenant; and thou shalt come into the ark, thou, and thy sons, and thy wife, and thy sons' wives with thee.

(19) And of every living thing of all flesh, two of every sort shalt thou bring into the ark, to keep them alive with thee; they shall be male and female.

(20) Of fowls after their kind, and of cattle after their kind, of every creeping thing of the earth after his kind, two of every sort shall come unto thee, to keep them alive.

(21) And take thou unto thee of all food that is eaten, and thou shalt gather it to thee; and it shall be for food for thee, and for them.

(22) Thus, did Noah; according to all that God commanded him, so did he.

All is fine and dandy now and God's plan is in full pattern. But is it and is what the bible reads correct? I read there are only 8 humans on the Ark and a bunch of animals. So where did the black skinned people come from? How about the yellow shinned people and the Kenites? How do you explain these people and where did they come from? I know they made it through the flood because they are still living on the earth at present time. Truly, I cannot answer these questions.

I can give some probabilities; one, when God said to Noah, "take two of all flesh" aboard the Ark, the other races are human and flesh, so they may have qualified and boarded the Ark. Two, perhaps the flood was not worldwide; it was only meant to get rid of all the hybrid giants from the mating of fallen angels with human women, and this goal wasn't completely achieved; Remember Goliath from the time of King David's reign? Three, Perhaps, Noah's sons were not blood sons; maybe he adopted a black man and woman and an oriental man and woman, thereby saving stock for future generations. And Four, maybe we don't have the exact SCRIPTURE as Moses wrote them down. Kenites are descendants of Cain and Cain's father was Satan; we know they made it through the flood, because they are mentioned in the book of Judges and also were still in the temple during Christ life as recorded in the book of John.

John 8:44

(44) Ye are of your father the devil, and the lusts of your father ye will do. He was a murderer from the beginning, and abode not in the truth, because there is no truth in him. When he speaketh a lie, he speaketh of his own: for he is a liar, and the father of it.

We are told the Kenites were working as scribes for the Levi's in the book of Chronicles.

1 Chronicles 2:55

(55) And the families of the scribes which dwelt at Jabez; the Tirathites, the Shimeathites, and Suchathites. These are the Kenites that came of Hemath, the father of the house of Rechab.

I'm thinking option #3 would probably be the best guess. What do you think?

Genesis 10:1-5 reads:

(1) Now these are the generations of the sons of Noah, Shem, Ham, and Japheth: and unto them were sons born after the flood.

(2) The sons of Japheth; Gomer, and Magog, and Madai, and Javan, and Tubal, and Meshech, and Tiras.

(3) And the sons of Gomer; Ashkenaz, and Riphath, and Togarmah.

(4) And the sons of Javan; Elishah, and Tarshish, Kittim, and Dodanim.

(5) By these were the isles of the Gentiles divided in their lands; everyone after his tongue, after their families, in their nations.

Perhaps, you noticed in the lineage of Japheth, several of his children have no offspring listed. Maybe I'm wrong, but several of these names appear in the nation of Russia and Mongolia in History books.

Ezekiel 38:6

(6) Gomer, and all his bands; the house of Togarmah of the north quarters, and all his bands: and many people with thee.

Ezekiel 38:2

(2) Son of man, set thy face against Gog, the land of Magog, the chief prince of Meshech and Tubal, and prophesy against him,

Ezekiel 27:13

(13) Javan, Tubal, and Meshech, they were thy merchants: they traded the persons of men and vessels of brass in thy market.

Ezekiel 32:26

(26) There is Meshech, Tubal, and all her multitude: her graves are round about him: all of them uncircumcised, slain by the sword, though they caused their terror in the land of the living.

Isaiah 66:19

(19) And I will set a sign among them, and I will send those that escape of them unto the nations, to Tarshish, Pul, and Lud, that draw the bow, to Tubal, and Javan, to the isles afar off, that have not heard my fame, neither have seen my glory; and they shall declare my glory among the Gentiles.

Genesis 4:22

(22) And Zillah, she also bare Tubalcain, an instructer of every artificer in brass and iron: and the sister of Tubalcain was Naamah.

Tubal-cain - Wikipedia

https://en.wikipedia.org/wiki/Tubal-cain

Tubal-cain or Tubalcain (Hebrew: תּוּבַל קַיִן –
Tūḇal Qáyin) is a person mentioned in the Bible, in
Genesis 4:22, known for being the first blacksmith. He
is stated as the "forger of all instruments of bronze
and iron". A descendant of Cain, he was the son of
Lamech and Zillah. Tubal-cain was the brother of
Naamah and half-brother of Jabal and Jubal. The
Israeli kibbutz, Tuval is named after him.

These are just some examples of why I think
the 'sons' of Noah were not blood related sons but
adopted sons for God to keep the Nations he created
intact. You may disagree with me and that's alright.
But the bible records the Kenites, (sons of Cain) lived
through the flood which according to the bible
destroyed all life that breathes air to live, unless they
were on the Ark with Noah. Also, we have the black
skinned people still on earth along with the Orientals.
If Noah and his three sons were blood relatives
(Adamic father and mother), these other Races
wouldn't exist.

I was raised on a farm and have dealt with all
types of breeding programs and breeding two of the

same individuals always gets the same type of individual.

Just a little bit more about the Earth being flooded during Noah's life.

Genesis 7:11

(11) In the six hundredth year of Noah's life, in the second month, the seventeenth day of the month, the same day were all the fountains of the great deep broken up, and the windows of heaven were opened. This verse let's us know that part of the ocean floor was ripped up and became part of the mountain range out West. That is, the Rocky Mountains in the U. S. and like so around the World. How do I know? All you have to do is look at the formation of these mountains. They are not pushed up from the ground from the shifting of the Teutonic plates on the earth but are layered like a brick mason would lay his bricks in building a structure.

Also, this time in our history is probably when the earth was pushed a little farther away from the sun. Now we have 365 & 1/4 days in a year when God's original creation only had 360 days to a year and before the flood, the bible tells us it had not rained on the earth but was watered by a mist rising each day to nourish all living creatures.

Genesis 2:5-6

(5) And every plant of the field before it was in the earth, and every herb of the field before it grew: for the LORD God had not caused it to rain upon the earth, and there was not a man to till the ground.

(6) But there went up a mist from the earth and watered the whole face of the ground.

Chapter 4

What's next? Well, there's not a whole lot of people on earth in the flesh at this time, so we'll just have to sit back and wait as God does while the people multiply and spread across the face of the earth.

So, while we wait, let's take a gander at some things you may not be aware of. I'm talking about all the Angels which used to live on the earth. We know God separated them; that is, the good (the ones who chose to support our Heavenly Father) from the bad (the ones who sided with Satan and tried to overthrow God and sit Satan on the Mercy seat).

God's word, the Bible, tells us he changed his angels into Spirits.

Psalms 104:4

Who makes his angels spirits, his ministers a flaming fire:

Are you surprised God changed all his Angels into Spirits? Well, he did, and I'm going to give you all the places in the bible where it talks bout spirits so you can read the article surrounding each event for yourself if you are that much interested. We'll find some are good, but most are the ones who followed Satan.

Leviticus 19:31

(31) Regard not them that have familiar spirits, neither seek after wizards, to be defiled by them: I am the LORD your God.

Leviticus (20:6)

(6) And the soul that turns after such as have familiar spirits, and after wizards, to go a whoring

after them, I will even set my face against that soul, and will cut him off from among his people.

Numbers 16:22

(22) And they fell upon their faces, and said, O God, the God of the spirits of all flesh, shall one-man sin, and wilt thou be mad with all the congregation?

Numbers 27:16

(16) Let the LORD, the God of the spirits of all flesh, set a man over the congregation,

Deuteronomy 18:11

(11) Or a charmer, or a consulter with familiar spirits, or a wizard, or a necromancer.

1 Samuel 28:3

(3) Now Samuel was dead, and all Israel had lamented him, and buried him in Ramah, even in his own city. And Saul had put away those that had familiar spirits, and the wizards, out of the land.

1 Samuel 28:9

(9) And the woman said unto him, Behold, thou know what Saul hath done, how he hath cut off those that have familiar spirits, and the wizards, out of the

land: wherefore then lay thou a snare for my life, to cause me to die?

2 Kings 21:6

(6) And he made his son pass through the fire, and observed times, and used enchantments, and dealt with familiar spirits and wizards: he wrought much wickedness in the sight of the LORD, to provoke him to anger.

2 Kings 23:24

(24) Moreover, the workers with familiar spirits, and the wizards, and the images, and the idols, and all the abominations that were spied in the land of Judah and in Jerusalem, did Josiah put away, that he might perform the words of the law which were written in the book that Hilkiah the priest found in the house of the LORD.

Psalms 104:4

(4) Who makes his angels spirits, his ministers a flaming fire:

Proverbs 16:2

(2) All the ways of a man are clean in his own eyes; but the LORD weighs the spirits.

Isaiah 8:19

(19) And when they shall say unto you, seek unto them that have familiar spirits, and unto wizards that peep, and that mutter: should not a people seek unto their God? for the living to the dead?

Isaiah 19:3

(3) And the spirit of Egypt shall fail in the midst thereof; and I will destroy the counsel thereof: and they shall seek to the idols, and to the charmers, and to them that have familiar spirits, and to the wizards.

Zechariah 6:5

(5) And the angel answered and said unto me, these are the four spirits of the heavens, which go forth from standing before the Lord of all the earth.

Matthew 8:16

(16) When the even was come, they brought unto him many that were possessed with devils: and he cast out the spirits with his word, and healed all that were sick:

Matthew 10:1

(1) And when he had called unto him his twelve disciples, he gave them power against unclean spirits,

to cast them out, and to heal all manner of sickness and all manner of disease.

Matthew 12:45

(45) Then he goes, and taketh with himself seven other spirits more wicked than himself, and they enter in and dwell there: and the last state of that man is worse than the first. Even so shall it be also unto this wicked generation.

Mark 1:27

(27) And they were all amazed, insomuch that they questioned among themselves, saying, what thing is this? what new doctrine is this? for with authority commands he even the unclean spirits, and they do obey him.

Mark 3:11

(11) And unclean spirits, when they saw him, fell down before him, and cried, saying, Thou art the Son of God.

Mark 5:13

(13) And forthwith Jesus gave them leave. And the unclean spirits went out and entered into the swine: and the herd ran violently down a steep place

into the sea, (they were about two thousand;) and were choked in the sea.

Mark 6:7

(7) And he called unto him the twelve and began to send them forth by two and two; and gave them power over unclean spirits.

Luke 4:36

(36) And they were all amazed, and spoke among themselves, saying, what a word is this! for with authority and power he commanded the unclean spirits, and they come out.

Luke 6:18

(18) And they that were vexed with unclean spirits: and they were healed.

Luke 7:21

(21) And in that same hour he cured many of their infirmities and plagues, and of evil spirits; and unto many that were blind he gave sight.

Luke 8:2

(2) And certain women, which had been healed of evil spirits and infirmities, Mary called Magdalene, out of whom went seven devils,

Luke 10:20

(20) Notwithstanding in this rejoice not, that the spirits are subject unto you; but rather rejoice, because your names are written in heaven.

Luke 11:26

(26) Then he goes, and taketh to him seven other spirits more wicked than himself; and they enter in, and dwell there: and the last state of that man is worse than the first.

Acts 5:16

(16) There also came a multitude out of the cities round about unto Jerusalem, bringing sick folks, and them which were vexed with unclean spirits: and they were healed everyone.

Acts 8:7

(7) For unclean spirits, crying with loud voice, came out of many that were possessed with them: and many taken with palsies, and that were lame, were healed.

Acts 19:12

(12) So that from his body were brought unto the sick handkerchiefs or aprons, and the diseases

departed from them, and the evil spirits went out of them.

Acts 19:13

(13) Then certain of the vagabond Jews, exorcists, took upon them to call over them which had evil spirits the name of the Lord Jesus, saying, we adjure you by Jesus whom Paul preaches.

1 Corinthians 12:10

(10) To another the working of miracles; to another prophecy; to another discerning of spirits; to another different kinds of tongues; to another the interpretation of tongues:

1 Corinthians 14:32

(32) And the spirits of the prophets are subject to the prophets.

1 Timothy 4:1

(1) Now the Spirit speaketh expressly, that in the latter times some shall depart from the faith, giving heed to seducing spirits, and doctrines of devils.

Hebrews 1:7

(7) And of the angels he saith, Who, make his angels spirits, and his ministers a flame of fire.

Hebrews 1:14

(14) Are they not all ministering spirits, sent forth to minister for them who shall be heirs of salvation?

Hebrews 12:9

(9) Furthermore, we have had fathers of our flesh which corrected us, and we gave them reverence: shall we not much rather be in subjection unto the Father of spirits, and live?

Hebrews 12:23

(23) To the general assembly and church of the firstborn, which are written in heaven, and to God the Judge of all, and to the spirits of just men made perfect,

1 Peter 3:19

(19) By which also he went and preached unto the spirits in prison.

1 John 4:1

(1) Beloved, believe not every spirit, but try the spirits whether they are of God: because many false prophets are gone out into the world.

Revelation 1:4

(4) John to the seven churches which are in Asia: Grace be unto you, and peace, from him which is, and which was, and which is to come; and from the seven Spirits which are before his throne.

Revelation 3:1

(1) And unto the angel of the church in Sardis write, these things saith he that hath the seven Spirits of God, and the seven stars; I know thy works, that thou hast a name that thou live, and art dead.

Revelation 4:5

(5) And out of the throne proceeded lightnings and thundering's and voices: and there were seven lamps of fire burning before the throne, which are the seven Spirits of God.

Revelation 5:6

(6) And I beheld, and, lo, in the midst of the throne and of the four beasts, and in the midst of the elders, stood a Lamb as it had been slain, having

seven horns and seven eyes, which are the seven Spirits of God sent forth into all the earth.

Revelation 16:13

(13) And I saw three unclean spirits like frogs come out of the mouth of the dragon, and out of the mouth of the beast, and out of the mouth of the false prophet.

Revelation 16:14

(14) For they are the spirits of devils, working miracles, which go forth unto the kings of the earth and of the whole world, to gather them to the battle of that great day of God Almighty.

Modern day prophets: Edgar Cayce.

Edgar Cayce is one of the most popular American Clairvoyants in history. Born on March 18, 1887. He is believed to have made predictions of future events ranging from wars, Atlantis, healing, and reincarnation while allegedly sleeping, which gave him the nickname, "The Sleeping Prophet".

Another prophet of modern times was Paul Solomon.

Paul Solomon - the other American "sleeping prophet" known internationally as a teacher, healer, minister, psychic, and humanitarian. He was nominated for his efforts particularly on behalf of the enslaved children and refugees of Thailand, for the Nobel Peace Prize in 1993.

I gave you these two "prophets" of modern times in order to show that prophets were not only in biblical days but are still with us today and have always existed with Humanity. You can research both of the two names on the internet if you are interested in knowing more about them.

Now, consider, in your opinion, did either of the two men, Edgar Cayce or Paul Salomon, have a familiar Spirit or fallen Spirit in them? I know you can't answer this question, I just wanted you to think for a moment.

It shows in the Bible, during the earthly life of Jesus the Christ, most spirits he removed from individuals were bad spirits or maybe at one time in their existence, had been followers of Satan in his rebellion against God.

But there is good news, Christ gave us, that is all of us who will use it, authority over all spirits. If you think there is a bad spirit in your life or of the life of a loved one; order it out. Just make sure you do it in Jesus name. They recognize Jesus' authority and will obey. But don't be like the men in Ephesus.

As stated in the book of Acts 19:13-16

(13) Then certain of the vagabond Jews, exorcists, took upon them to call over them which had evil spirits the name of the Lord Jesus, saying, we adjure you by Jesus whom Paul preaches.

(14) And there were seven sons of one Sceva, a Jew, and chief of the priests, which did so.

(15) And the evil spirit answered and said, Jesus I know, and Paul I know; but who are ye?

(16) And the man in whom the evil spirit was leaped on them, and overcame them, and prevailed against them, so that they fled out of that house naked and wounded.

You can't handle a familiar spirit on your own; the authority Jesus gave you is no good if you try to set yourself up as some kind of exorcist. These spirits will beat you to a pulp as they did to the idiots in Ephesus during Apostle Paul's time. God has already placed a spirit of one of his children (Angel) in your body at conception of your birth. I don't think he wants any other spirit messing your mind up. Just my thinking from what I've read in the bible.

Ok, enough about Spirits for the time being. We left off in our discussion at the end of the flood during Noah's lifetime on earth. What happens next? We read about two of Noah's sons, (Japhet and Ham) multiplying and scattering their offspring all over the known earth as God watches and is pleased, that is, all except Nimrod, one of the grandsons of Ham. Nimrod is a mighty hunter and builds cities that he can rule in the plains of Shinar. As it reads in Genesis 10:8-10:

(8) And Cush begat Nimrod: he began to be a mighty one in the earth.

(9) He was a mighty hunter before the LORD: wherefore it is said, Even as Nimrod the mighty hunter before the LORD.

(10) And the beginning of his kingdom was Babel, and Erech, and Accad, and Calneh, in the land of Shinar.

Why was God not pleased with Nimrod? He stayed in one location and decided to do things his way, therefore, ignoring God.

In the above scripture given that Nimrod was a mighty hunter is a bit misleading. The actual translation in the Hebrew tells us Nimrod was a mighty adversary before God. It seems he listen to the wrong voice and decided he wanted to rule his brothers and sisters instead of helping them.

The KJV bible doesn't tell us exactly that Nimrod built the Tower of Babel, but in the book of Jubilees, it does and a lot more.

The Book of Jubilees contains one of the most detailed accounts found anywhere of the Tower.

And they began to build, and in the fourth week they made brick with fire, and the bricks served them for stone, and the clay with which they cemented them together was asphalt which comes out of the sea, and out of the fountains of water in the land of

Shinar. And they built it: forty and three years were they building it; its breadth was 203 bricks, and the height [of a brick] was the third of one; its height amounted...

I guess right about now you are wondering what does the book of Jubilees have to do with the history of God's people and why do I think it is important? Fair question: but first, why do you trust the KJV of the bible to be true? In case you didn't know, the Catholic Church had sole control over what was in the bible for 1260 years? That's right, 1260 years, from 538 AD until 1798 AD. But you say, the KJV was published in 1611 AD, and you are right. Do you know where the scriptures were taken the translators used? I'll give you a hint; there was only one bible available at the time. The Catholic Bible. So, what was the problem with using that Catholic bible: it was written in Latin and the average person on the street didn't understand the Latin language. As far as society was concerned, Latin was a dead language. That was what all the hullabaloo was all about and of course, the

Catholic Church forbid anybody to own a copy of the bible unless they belong to the Catholic priesthood.

Chapter 5

What' next on God's agenda? After confusing
the same language of the people at the Tower of
Babel; God scatters these people into all parts of the
earth. Keep in mind, God knows which spirit of his
Angelic sons he puts into each flesh body. I'm sure at
this time God is watching a man called Abram who
seems to have all of the qualifications our Lord wants
in a human man to continue to use to bring himself
(Jesus) into this flesh world as a redeemer for Adam's
original sin which causes all flesh man to need a
sacrifice be paid to bring them back into the good
graces of our Heavenly Father. God knows which spirit

is placed into Abram, but Abram still needs to be tested in order to find out if the flesh will change his thinking and cause him to love the worldly pleasures more than God.

Abram moves with his family, that is, his earthly father, Haran, from the city of Ur to Haran as given in Genesis 11:26-31

(26) And Terah lived seventy years, and begat Abram, Nahor, and Haran.

(27) Now these are the generations of Terah: Terah begat Abram, Nahor, and Haran; and Haran begat Lot.

(28) And Haran died before his father Terah in the land of his nativity, in Ur of the Chaldees.

(29) And Abram and Nahor took them wives: the name of Abram's wife was Sarai; and the name of Nahor's wife, Milcah, the daughter of Haran, the father of Milcah, and the father of Iscah.

(30) But Sarai was barren; she had no child.

(31) And Terah took Abram his son, and Lot the son of Haran his son's son, and Sarai his daughter in law, his son Abram's wife; and they went forth with

them from Ur of the Chaldees, to go into the land of Canaan; and they came unto Haran and dwelt there.

At this time in Abram's life, he is about 75 years of age. He has married his half-sister; Abram and his wife Sari, have the same father but different mothers. At this time in history, it was common for sons and daughter of the same family to engage in wedlock.

It was while Abram was living in Haran, God told Abram to leave his kinfolk and move to a land he would be shown by God. Abram took his wife and all the property he had accumulated and moved as God ordered. As stated in Genesis 12:1-5

(1) Now the LORD had said unto Abram, get thee out of thy country, and from thy kindred, and from thy father's house, unto a land that I will show thee:

(2) And I will make of thee a great nation, and I will bless thee, and make thy name great; and thou shalt be a blessing:

(3) And I will bless them that bless thee and curse him that curses thee: and in thee shall all families of the earth be blessed.

(4) So, Abram departed, as the LORD had spoken unto him; and Lot went with him: and Abram was seventy and five years old when he departed out of Haran.

(5) And Abram took Sarai his wife, and Lot his brother's son, and all their substance that they had gathered, and the souls that they had gotten in Haran; and they went forth to go into the land of Canaan; and into the land of Canaan, they came.

We all know the story of Abram and why God changed his name to Abraham and blessed him and promised him that by changing his name to Abraham, he would be Father to many nations. History has shown us who are living several thousand years later; Abraham has many descendants and multi nations have sprung from his loins. Maybe you are wondering why God blessed Abraham so? Perhaps, it was the sacrifice he was willing to make to his heavenly father.

In case you have forgotten or never was told, this is why God chose Abraham.

Abraham and Sarah had been childless all their lives and now Abraham final sired a son, Isaiah, when he was 100 years of age and his wife, Sarah, was 90 years in age. Both were too old to bear children naturally, so this child was the work of the Holy Spirit of God.

Genesis 22:1-18

(1) And it came to pass after these things, that God did tempt Abraham, and said unto him, Abraham: and he said, Behold, here I am.

(2) And he said, take now thy son, thine only son Isaac, whom thou love, and get thee into the land of Moriah; and offer him there for a burnt offering upon one of the mountains which I will tell thee of.

(3) And Abraham rose up early in the morning, and saddled his ass, and took two of his young men with him, and Isaac his son, and clave the wood for the burnt offering, and rose up, and went unto the place of which God had told him.

(4) Then on the third day Abraham lifted up his eyes and saw the place afar off.

(5) And Abraham said unto his young men, abide ye here with the ass; and I and the lad will go yonder and worship, and come again to you.

(6) And Abraham took the wood of the burnt offering and laid it upon Isaac his son; and he took the fire in his hand, and a knife; and they went both of them together.

(7) And Isaac spoke unto Abraham his father, and said, my father: and he said, here am I, my son. And he said, Behold the fire and the wood: but where is the lamb for a burnt offering?

(8) And Abraham said, my son, God will provide himself a lamb for a burnt offering: so, they went both of them together.

(9) And they came to the place which God had told him of; and Abraham built an altar there, and laid the wood in order, and bound Isaac his son, and laid him on the altar upon the wood.

(10) And Abraham stretched forth his hand and took the knife to slay his son.

(11) And the angel of the LORD called unto him out of heaven, and said, Abraham, Abraham: and he said, here am I.

(12) And he said, lay not thine hand upon the lad, neither do thou anything unto him: for now, I know that thou fear God, seeing thou hast not withheld thy son, thine only son from me.

(13) And Abraham lifted up his eyes, and looked, and behold behind him a ram caught in a thicket by his horns: and Abraham went and took the ram and offered him up for a burnt offering in the stead of his son.

(14) And Abraham called the name of that place Jehovahjireh: as it is said to this day, In the mount of the LORD it shall be seen.

(15) And the angel of the LORD called unto Abraham out of heaven the second time,

(16) And said, by myself have I sworn, saith the LORD, for because thou hast done this thing, and hast not withheld thy son, thine only son:

(17) That in blessing I will bless thee, and in multiplying I will multiply thy seed as the stars of the

heaven, and as the sand which is upon the seashore; and thy seed shall possess the gate of his enemies.

(18) And in thy seed shall all the nations of the earth be blessed because thou hast obeyed my voice.

I wanted to include this part about Abraham's faith to God. Think about it; Abraham waited 100 years for a child and when God made it possible for his wife Sarah to conceive a child, God waited until the child was old enough to reach the age of accountability, God told Abraham, he wanted the child sacrificed to him. What would you do? What did Abraham do? Abraham obeyed God! He had faith to believe if God wanted this child, it would be the best thing for the child, which was not a child any longer, but a young man of accountability. Why is this important? I think the young man had as much say so in the matter as his earthly father. And what did the young man do when he realized he was to be the sacrifice? He didn't resist; he complied with his earthly father's wish.

This is important because years later Jesus would make the same choice. The young son in the story of Abraham was Issacs and he loved his earthly father to want of obey his every wish. Jesus loved his Heavenly father and wanted to obey his every wish. This is the reason God chose Abraham; do you understand what you have just read?

God, our Heavenly Father loves us enough, his children, whether we are good or bad, to die for us; to replace our sins with his blood; that is if we repent of what our sins are! Think about this!

So, now we come to David and Bathsheba and God's chosen people are messing up again.

Our story starts with David staying behind when his army goes to war. One afternoon after awaking from his nap, David walked across the roof of the king's house and saw a beautiful woman washing herself. (2 Samuel 11:2) Now if we look at this event as Hollywood did in the famous movie, we picture a nude woman at her bath. This imagery will bring forth desire in any man and most readers of the bible accept this as the way David saw Bathsheba; but was this really what was going on. Already, we have a few errors; first the bible doesn't say anything about

Bathsheba being "naked", does it? Next, what does the Hebrew word translated "beautiful" really mean? The word is "towb" (tobe) and means beautiful alright; but when you read the rest of the meanings and information given in the Strong's Concordance, it quickly comes to mind, the writer is describing the "inside" of a person. Bathsheba was a "good" person; one whom gave joy to all who came into contact with her. Her personality radiated joy and trust to everybody. Her face could have stopped an eight-day clock; but nobody would see this side of her, only the inner glow which spread everywhere she went. Now, I didn't say she had an ugly face; I said if she did have one, nobody would notice it. For you to really get a good picture in your mind of the person Bathsheba was, I'm going to give the many meanings of the word "towb". (good in the widest sense; a good thing; good man or woman; beautiful; best; better; bountiful; cheerful; at ease; favor; fine; glad; graciously; joyful; kindly; kindness; like; loving; mercy; pleasant; precious; sweet) Now I may have left out a couple, but I think you get the idea. She wasn't in her courtyard stripped naked to seduce David or any other man. The custom was for a woman to take a "spit bath" during the daytime, which means washing under her arms and private parts with her clothes on. Ask your wife or girlfriend; they'll explain what I'm describing.

Why did David send for her? Like I said above, her personality was such to where all people desired to be in her presence. David was no different; I'm sure he already knew who she was, her grandfather being one of the priests in the temple. Perhaps you think I'm trying to whitewash their sin? I'm not! I only want to show you how Satan works in everybody's life. David and Bathsheba's sins were very great, and they paid a hard price.

After the sin of adultery was committed, what happens next? Bathsheba informs David she is with child. (2 Sam. 11:5) Notice, she didn't say she was with child by David; but only "I am with child". Was the child David's or her husband, Uriah? I don't think Bathsheba knew herself. It hadn't been that long since her husband had gone to war. Now, most bible critic's use the phrase "for she was purified from her uncleanness" to mean she was passed her menstrual cycle and was ripe for pregnancy. This could or could not be true. There were lots of duties to be performed at the Temple and purification rites were standard for the people. She could have been purified from a religious duty. Nobody will know for sure. The facts remain in that she was pregnant, and David took responsibility for the child. Next, David had her husband, Uriah murdered. WOW! Another fatal sin: both sins carried the death penalty. David had broken two of God's commandants; (Exodus 20:13; 20:14) so, why didn't God remove his "Holy Spirit" from David as he had from Saul? Does God play favorites? No, of course not; to start with, David asked for forgiveness when he was confronted with his sin and Saul never did. (2 Samuel 12:13) Saul considered himself "above the law". He was the king of Israel and answered to no law; he made the law. Sort of like a lot of our politicians today, right!

Before you start thinking God was a little too lenient with David, let's take a look at Uriah and just who he was. The bible always mentions Uriah was a Hittite in speaking of his person. WHY? Let's turn the pages of the bible back a few years and see who the Hittites are. They are first brought to light in the book of Genesis. (Gen. 15:20) They are among the tribes who have infested the land of Canaan where God has told Abraham he can have all the land his eyes can see. To be blunt; these are the tribes which have been infected with another influx of "fallen angels". These are the tribes God told Joshua to utterly destroy, for he was going to give Israel all of the land they lived in. (Joshua 1:4) These people are the tribes from which the "giants" David and his Nephews killed, came from.

We don't know how or why Uriah came to be in the camp of David; we are not told in the bible. But what was the trademark of the "fallen angel" offspring. Some were giants; some were gay as the inhabitants of Sodom and Gomorrah; none had a spirit of one of God's children placed in them. (Isa. 26:13, 14, & 19) "O Lord our God, other lords beside thee have had dominion over us: but by thee only will we make mention of thy name. They are dead, they shall not live; they are deceased, they shall not rise, therefore, hast thou visited and destroyed them, and made all their memory to perish." The English translation loses part of the meaning of God's word. The words "they are" have been added in verse 14. This verse should read, "dead, they shall not live; repaired, they shall not rise:" The word "deceased" is not among the different meanings for the Hebrew word "Rapha." I could have used "cured; healed; mended; but not deceased because it is not among the different meanings given that this word could be translated into. I could have not translated it at all and left the word as it was given in the manuscripts. The Hebrew word is "Rapha" and transliterated instead of translating, the word is the name of one of the tribes of Giants God wanted destroyed out of Canaan. If we return to the subject being discussed, "other lords", we readily see people are being discussed; the Rephaims. They are the "other lords". God's word says they cannot be healed or cured or repaired. Why? They are hybrids, born of the fallen angel influx and the daughters of Adam. God has not placed the "soul" of one of his children from the 1st earth age into their bodies. Skip down to verse 19 of this same chapter, "Thy dead men shall live, ("men" has been added) together with my dead body shall they rise. ("together with" has been added) Awake and sing, ye that dwell in dust; for thy dew is as the dew of herbs, and the earth shall cast out the dead." Dead is a mistranslation; the correct translation is "flabby thing". My Hebrew is not great, but God thru the scribe who penned this book of Isaiah is saying his people shall live and their spirits will rise with a new body at the time of physical death. (Eccl. 12:7) Also, the hybrids will not live because they have no spirit to rise. (earth will cast out the flabby thing)

We know Uriah was a great warrior because he is listed among David's "mighty men"; but being a great soldier doesn't preclude him from being gay. One thing for certain, his heritage carried the blood of fallen angels.

Take another look at the events which surrounded Uriah's "three-day pass" from the battlefield. Anybody who has been in combat or just watched movies about combat troops knows what is expected when a soldier goes on "R&R". (rest and relaxation). They are to, "let their hair down" a bit; enjoy the company of their wife or girlfriend; whatever it takes to take their mind off the war. So, it was with Uriah! What happened? He slept with David's servants, (2 Samuel 11:9) and gave the excuse he couldn't have a good time while his fellow troops were on the front lines. (2 Samuel 11:11) Hogwash! I believe he was gay and wanted to be with men! Even when David got him drunk, he still "went out to lie on his bed with the servants"; he wasn't interested in his wife. This in my opinion is the reason Bathsheba was so susceptible to David's advances.

Now, if you accept my opinion that Uriah was gay and of the bunch God had already condemned; why did God get so mad at David having him killed? Because he was not carrying out God's sentence on those tribes; but was murdering a personal human being. Also, in doing this thing and taking Bathsheba for his wife, there would always be rumors about who was the real father of the child in Bathsheba's womb? Remember, David and Bathsheba were of the elect of God to do special things in this 2nd earth age to keep progress as God wanted it. To correct the situation, God took the life of the baby. You see, this was the bloodline Christ was to come through and God would not let a speck of gossip about a pure descent from Adam enter into the picture.

Circumstances didn't have to happen the way they did. God told David through the prophet Nathan that he could have anything he wanted. He had already given him a kingdom and Saul's wives and if that had not been enough, he would have given him anything his heart desired. (2 Samuel 12:8) All David had to do was ask God for it! (I threw some of this in so you can see how Satan works in this age)

How about the child God condemned to death? We are told in Ezekiel God doesn't hold the sins of the father against the child and the sins of the child against the father. Everybody stands or falls on what they do in this life. (Ezek. 18:2) As a matter of fact, the whole chapter 18 in the book of Ezekiel tells us how God judges his people. So, what has this baby of Bathsheba's done to warrant death? We have already talked about the pedigree of Christ; but God wouldn't kill a child just for this reason. Remember God loves his children; he destroyed a whole earth age to keep from killing his children. If this pedigree thing were the only reason, God would have disowned David's line and used another. So there has to be something else. When we take a look at the words "die" in verses 13 and 14, (2 Samuel 12:13 & 14) we find the Hebrew is the same word for both our English words, "die". The word in the Hebrew is "muwth" and means to die alright; but God here is referring to spiritual death. God is saying David is not worthy of spiritual death. Why? Because David had already earned eternal life in the 1st earth age and in this 2nd earth age, he is being used of God to carry out God's will. All right! What about the baby? God said the baby "shall surely die" meaning the baby is worthy of spiritual death or when the flesh dies, there's nothing left. THE BABY WAS URIAH'S CHILD AND HAD "FALLEN ANGEL" BLOOD IN HIM. This and only this is the reason God condemned him to death. Because of the angel blood mixed in the child, God said this would give God's enemies occasion to blaspheme his name.

God will not allow his name to be blasphemed! "Thou have greatly blasphemed the Lord" is the correct translation of the last part of verse 14 instead of "thou hast given great occasion to the enemies of the Lord to blaspheme". David's was the one who blasphemed the Lord by his actions. This is noted in the MASSORAH as one of the emendations of the SOPHERIM, who alter the primitive text out of a mistaken reverence for JHVH and David. (p.423; Companion Bible; for a further study on the MASSORAH and the SOPHERIM, see appendix 30 & 33 of the same bible) Even with this mistranslation, the facts still remain. God does not hold the sin of the father against the children born. Look at Jacob and Essau; God said he hated Essau before he was born; but Essau's life and heritage in this 2nd earth age was dependent on what Essau did with what God gave him at the start. Like the parable of the ten talents, Jesus gave; God looks at how you use your gifts. What does God have to say about this subject in the book of Jeremiah? "But ever one shall die for his own iniquity: every man that eateth the sour grape, his teeth shall be set on edge." (Jeremiah 31:30) The baby had to die because of the fallen angel blood in its veins the same as the sons of Judah who were by the Canaanite woman, Shuah. (Gen. 38:7-10) The Canaanites were one of the tribes infected with "fallen Angel" blood and the descendants of Abraham were forbidden to enter into a marriage relation with this tribe, or any of the tribes mentioned in this part of the bible. (Gen. 24:3; Duet. 7:1-3) Bathsheba was already in "Dutch" with our Lord because she was already married into this line of "fallen angel" descendants, the Hittites. Mind you, God wouldn't have interfered in Bathsheba's life if David hadn't taken her for his wife. When this happened, God's plan for the birth of Christ was in jeopardy. This, God wouldn't allow; he had already destroyed this world by a flood to keep this from happening during the days of Noah. (Gen. 7:10-24)

For this reason the child was destroyed and not because of the sins of David and Bathsheba.

To mix your blood with the blood of a fallen angel is blasphemous to our Father. (have sex with a fallen angel and have children). I'm warning you now because in the near future, these angels of a fallen nature will once again walk the earth in bodily form seducing all who will listen to their lies of seduction. (Rev. 12:7-9; Jude 1:16-19) Satan will be leading them claiming to be the "Christ" and will deceive "all" but God's "elect". Don't be deceived; Christ will not come until after Satan has set up his kingdom here on earth and ruled for a short time. (five months; Rev. 9:5) Then Christ will come at the last trump. (Rev. 10:7) How many trumps are there? Seven trumps in all; Christ will come at the seventh trump. Satan will come at the six trump, (666- 6th seal, 6th vial, 6th trump) claiming to be Christ. DON'T BE DECEIVED!

I wanted to give my version of the biblical story of David and Bathsheba because God said David was a man after his own heart. When the New Testament writers address Jesus, they all referred to him being the son of David. How much praise can you give to a mortal man than to have the son of God be addressed as a son of David while in the flesh?

Matthew 1:1

(1) The book of the generation of Jesus Christ, the son of David, the son of Abraham.

This is how the gospel of Matthew begins. But to be classified with being an ancestor of Jesus Christ and then to Abraham is truly marvelous. We know from the article I wrote about David that he was not a perfect man without sin, so what was his secret for God to love him so much? It's really simple and it's the same thing God wants from all of his children. David put God first in his life; when he messed up and committed sin in God's eyes, he didn't try to hide it or blame other people, (like Adam did in the Garden of Eden when confronted by God for his disobedience) but said I'm guilty and whatever punishment God called for, David took it in stride and asked God for forgiveness. Throughout David's mortal life, he never lost his faith and trust in our Heavenly Father.

Most of the 'Old Testament' is God dealing with his children's disobedience and what he did time and time again to correct them and set them on the right path again. Finally, God got fed up with his wayward children and let their enemies overtake them and allowed them to be scattered over the face of the earth. Still, God watched over them and without their knowing it, he would help them a little bit.

Nehemiah 1:8

(8) Remember, I beseech thee, the word that thou commanded thy servant Moses, saying, if ye transgress, I will scatter you abroad among the nations:

Jeremiah 9:16

(16) I will scatter them also among the heathen, whom neither they nor their fathers have known, and I will send a sword after them, till I have consumed them.

Ezekiel 20:34

(34) And I will bring you out from the people and will gather you out of the countries wherein ye

are scattered, with a mighty hand, and with a stretched-out arm, and with fury poured out.

John 11:52

(52) And not for that nation only, but that also he should gather together in one the children of God that were scattered abroad.

James 1:1

(1) James, a servant of God and of the Lord Jesus Christ, to the twelve tribes which are scattered abroad, greeting.

So, where are the children of Israel? God scattered them over the earth like he said he would.

What parent hasn't watched their children make wrong decisions and bad choses and cried inwardly and outwardly for their children to change their ways and live as God would have them live. Now, perhaps you can begin to understand how God feels about his children who won't listen to him and insist on doing things their own way.

Chapter 6

Right! God's children wanted to do things on their own; so now God let's them. The Assyrian Army conquers the 10 northern tribes of Israel, who by the way are calling themselves the Nation of Israel. God has scattered or removed them out of his sight. And almost 200 years later, God sends Nebuchadnezzar to conquer the remaining tribes left in the land God gave to Abraham. What happened to them? They went the same way the 10 tribes to the North went, that is, breaking God's covenant and laws, until he became fed up with them as he did the 10 tribes of Israel. But what now? We know God promised to bring a savior to redeem the world and make a sacrifice to pay for the sins of all the people who would repent of their sins and ask for forgiveness. Is this promise now forgotten? No! God doesn't forget anything unless he choses too. So how will God keep his promise?

Daniel 1:1-7

(1) In the third year of the reign of Jehoiakim king of Judah came Nebuchadnezzar king of Babylon unto Jerusalem and besieged it.

(2) And the Lord gave Jehoiakim king of Judah into his hand, with part of the vessels of the house of God: which he carried into the land of Shinar to the house of his god; and he brought the vessels into the treasure house of his god.

(3) And the king spoke unto Ashpenaz the master of his eunuchs, that he should bring certain of the children of Israel, and of the king's seed, and of the princes,

(4) Children in whom was no blemish, but well favored, and skillful in all wisdom, and cunning in knowledge, and understanding science, and such as had ability in them to stand in the king's palace, and

whom they might teach the learning and the tongue of the Chaldeans.

(5) And the king appointed them a daily provision of the king's meat, and of the wine which he drank: so, nourishing them three years, that at the end thereof they might stand before the king.

(6) Now among these were of the children of Judah, Daniel, Hananiah, Mishael, and Azariah:

(7) Unto whom the prince of the eunuchs gave names: for he gave unto Daniel the name of Belteshazzar; and to Hananiah, of Shadrach; and to Mishael, of Meshach; and to Azariah, of Abednego.

Now we know how Daniel was placed into Nebuchadnezzar court and next we see why. In order for Nebuchadnezzar to understand the power of the Creator, God gave him a dream and then made him forget what the dream was so he would call his magicians to tell him the dream and what it meant. Of course, they couldn't do either of the two things the king demanded of them. Only God can read minds. Finally, Daniel arrives on the scene and tells the king, there is a God in heaven who will show Nebuchadnezzar his dream and the meaning of it. Notice Daniel didn't claim to have any special talents in the revealing of dreams, only God can do what the king wanted. This is the dream:

Daniel 2:2

(2) Then the king commanded to call the magicians, and the astrologers, and the sorcerers, and the Chaldeans, for to shew the king his dreams. So, they came and stood before the king.

(3) And the king said unto them, I have dreamed a dream, and my spirit was troubled to know the dream.

(4) Then spoke the Chaldeans to the king in Syriack, O king, live forever: tell thy servants the dream, and we will shew the interpretation.

(5) The king answered and said to the Chaldeans, the thing is gone from me: if ye will not make known unto me the dream, with the interpretation thereof, ye shall be cut in pieces, and your houses shall be made a dunghill.

(6) But if ye shew the dream, and the interpretation thereof, ye shall receive of me gifts and rewards and great honor: therefore, shew me the dream, and the interpretation thereof.

(7) They answered again and said, Let the king tell his servants the dream, and we will shew the interpretation of it.

(8) The king answered and said, I know of certainty that ye would gain the time, because ye see the thing is gone from me.

(9) But if ye will not make known unto me the dream, there is but one decree for you: for ye have prepared lying and corrupt words to speak before me, till the time be changed: therefore, tell me the dream, and I shall know that ye can shew me the interpretation thereof.

(10) The Chaldeans answered before the king, and said, there is not a man upon the earth that can shew the king's matter: therefore, there is no king, lord, nor ruler, that asked such things at any magician, or astrologer, or Chaldean.

When Daniel hears the decree, the King has ordered all the magicians, astrologers, and Chaldean to be put to death if they cannot do what King Nebuchadnezzar wants to be put to death, he asks for time to ask God for the interpretation of the King's dream. God honors his request and Daniel goes before the King and tells him what God has given to Daniel.

Daniel Chapter 2: 31-45

(31) Thou, O king, sawest, and behold a great image. This great image, whose brightness was excellent, stood before thee; and the form thereof was terrible.

(32) This image's head was of fine gold, his breast and his arms of silver, his belly, and his thighs of brass,

(33) His legs of iron, his feet part of iron and part of clay.

(34) Thou sawest till that a stone was cut out without hands, which smote the image upon his feet that were of iron and clay, and brake them to pieces.

(35) Then was the iron, the clay, the brass, the silver, and the gold, broken to pieces together, and became like the chaff of the summer threshing floors; and the wind carried them away, that no place was found for them: and the stone that smote the image became a great mountain, and filled the whole earth.

(36) This is the dream; and we will tell the interpretation thereof before the king.

(37) Thou, O king, art a king of kings: for the God of heaven hath given thee a kingdom, power, and strength, and glory.

(38) And wheresoever the children of men dwell, the beasts of the field and the fowls of the heaven hath he given into thine hand, and hath made thee ruler over them all. Thou art this head of gold.

(39) And after you, there shall arise another kingdom inferior to thee, and another third kingdom of brass, which shall bear rule over all the earth.

(40) And the fourth kingdom shall be strong as iron: forasmuch as iron breaks in pieces and subdues all things: and as iron that breaks all these, shall it break in pieces and bruise.

(41) And whereas thou sawest the feet and toes, part of potters' clay, and part of iron, the kingdom shall be divided; but there shall be in it of the strength of the iron, forasmuch as thou sawest the iron mixed with miry clay.

(42) And as the toes of the feet were part of iron, and part of clay, so the kingdom shall be partly strong, and partly broken.

(43) And whereas thou sawest iron mixed with miry clay, they shall mingle themselves with the seed of men: but they shall not cleave one to another, even as iron is not mixed with clay.

(44) And in the days of these kings shall the God of heaven set up a kingdom, which shall never be destroyed: and the kingdom shall not be left to other people, but it shall break in pieces and consume all these kingdoms, and it shall stand for ever.

(45) Forasmuch as thou sawest that the stone was cut out of the mountain without hands, and that it breaks in pieces the iron, the brass, the clay, the silver, and the gold; the great God hath made known

to the king what shall come to pass hereafter: and the dream is certain, and the interpretation thereof sure.

History shows us the Babylonia, under Nebuchadnezzar was the first kingdom and the Medes-Persians, the second empire. The third was the Greeks under the leadership of Alexander the Great. The fourth was Rome, and it lasted past the time Jesus walked the earth in the flesh.

But, what about the kingdom God said he would set up in the days of these kings which would last forever and never be destroyed? Where is it? Why do we not see it, if God did set up this kingdom?

What did Jesus tell Pilate when he was questioned about this Kingdom?

Mark 15:2

(2) And Pilate asked him, Art thou the King of the Jews? And he answers, and said unto him, Thou sayest it.

(26) And the superscription of his accusation was written over, THE KING OF THE JEWS.

John 18:36

(36) Jesus answered, my kingdom is not of this world: if my kingdom were of this world, then would my servants fight, that I should not be delivered to the Jews: but now is my kingdom not from hence.

Do you understand what you have just read? God set up a kingdom just as he said he would in the book of Daniel, but it's not of this flesh world. It is being set-up in Heaven. Our Savior, Jesus, came into this flesh world as a baby and when the time was right, he paid the sin debt created by Adam in the 'Garden of Eden' and now all the children of God who repent of the evil they have done in this flesh age can now be forgiven and become part of this Kingdom Christ is setting up in Heaven. I'm sure you haven't realized it before now, but all souls of the people who died in the flesh before Christ paid the sin debt have been locked up in the prison across the vast gulf where the rich man in the parable of 'Lazarus and the Rich man', Christ gave in his teaching.

So, what do you think Christ did as soon as he died on the cross? Perhaps, you have been taught he returned to the Father. Well, if you were, you were taught wrong. What does the bible really tell us?

1 Peter 4:6

(6) For this cause was the gospel preached also to them that are dead, that they might be judged according to men in the flesh but live according to God in the spirit.

Where are the dead, Christ preached too? I just told you a few paragraphs above; they are the ones held across the vast gulf in Heaven where the Rich Man is being held. Got that! What happened when Christ preached to this bunch of dead souls?

We'll find our answer in the Gospel of Matthew.

Matthew 27:50-53

(50) Jesus, when he had cried again with a loud voice, yielded up the ghost.

(51) And behold, the veil of the temple was rent in twain from the top to the bottom; and the earth did quake, and the rocks rent.

(52) And the graves were opened; and many bodies of the saints which slept arose,

(53) And came out of the graves after his resurrection, and went into the holy city, and appeared unto many.

The graves are in heaven where the 'rich Man' is held, not in some earthly cemetery out behind some church. There is nothing in these earthly graves but some rotting bones and perhaps some worm-eaten clothes the person was buried in. You don't agree with me? That's ok, will you agree with what the bible says or you going to keep listening to idiot preachers and believe in traditions handed down by ignorant people?

Ecclesiastes 12;6-7

(6) Or ever the silver cord be loosed, or the golden bowl be broken, or the pitcher be broken at the fountain, or the wheel broken at the cistern.

(7) Then shall the dust return to the earth as it was: and the spirit shall return unto God who gave it.

Where does the spirit go when you die? It returns unto God who gave you the spirit. You have studied Paul's teachings in the New Testament, haven't you? What does he say on the subject?

1 Corinthians 15:50-55

(50) Now this I say, brethren, that flesh and blood cannot inherit the kingdom of God; neither doth corruption inherit incorruption.

(51) Behold, I shew you a mystery; We shall not all sleep, but we shall all be changed,

(52) In a moment, in the twinkling of an eye, at the last trump: for the trumpet shall sound, and the dead shall be raised incorruptible, and we shall be changed.

(53) For this corruptible must put on incorruption, and this mortal must put on immortality.

(54) So, when this corruptible shall have put on incorruption, and this mortal shall have put on

immortality, then shall be brought to pass the saying that is written, Death is swallowed up in victory.

(55) O death, where is thy sting? O grave, where is thy victory?

1 Peter 3:18

(18) For Christ also hath once suffered for sins, the just for the unjust, that he might bring us to God, being put to death in the flesh, but quickened by the Spirit:

And what else did Christ do after the crucifixion? Oh, he didn't forget about the Angelic Spirits who disobeyed his command to leave the physical world or Age alone. You remember the spirits whom Christ commanded to come out of certain people he met while walking this earth in a physical form.

Jude 1:6

(6) And the angels which kept not their first estate, but left their own habitation, he hath reserved in everlasting chains under darkness unto the judgment of the great day.

Christ visited these same spirits in the prison where he had them locked up in chains. And what did he do when he visited them?

1 Peter 3:19

(19) By which also he went and preached unto the spirits in prison.

The verse should have been translated 'heralded' instead of 'preached' even though the Greek is correct using either word. My opinion, Christ shouted what he had accomplished to this bunch in prison because they didn't believe he could come into the flesh world and die on the cross as a sacrifice without committing a sin. These had worked with Satan to stop him from doing this and they failed.

We have a little more to learn from the Book of Daniel before we leave off some of its prophecies.

Daniel 7:3-27

(3) And four great beasts came up from the sea, diverse one from another.

Keep in mind when the bible gives images, they represent something beside what is written. Like this word 'sea', we are told waters are people. Here we are told about four beasts coming out of the 'sea'. This means coming from the people.

(4) The first was like a lion and had eagle's wings: I beheld till the wings thereof were plucked, and it was lifted up from the earth, and made stand upon the feet as a man, and a man's heart was given to it.

This lion with wings represents King Nebuchadnezzar. The winged lion was painted on much of the walls built around the city of Babylon.

(5) And behold another beast, a second, like to a bear, and it raised up itself on one side, and it had three ribs in the mouth of it between the teeth of it: and they said thus unto it, Arise, devour much flesh.

This is Medo-Persia; same images we had in chapter 2, almost, but maybe a little different, but the same kingdoms are represented.

(6) After this I beheld, and lo another, like a leopard, which had upon the back of it four wings of a fowl; the beast had also four heads; and dominion was given to it.

This is the Greek empire under Alexander the Great. The four heads represent the four territories his kingdom would be divided into after his death.

(7) After this I saw in the night visions, and behold a fourth beast, dreadful and terrible, and strong exceedingly; and it had great iron teeth: it devoured and brake in pieces and stamped the residue with the feet of it: and it was diverse from all the beasts that were before it; and it had ten horns.

This is the Roman Empire; just a little more detail and something about the peoples round about Rome. The Horns in prophetic messages always portray power or Nations. In this case, the horns are representative of the barbaric tribes which came through the Caucasian Mountain and settled what is now Europe. These tribes are the remnants of the 10 tribes of Israel after they left the bondage of Assyrian Empire. These peoples were called Caucasian, because of their travels across the Caucasus Mountain. This is the reason white skinned people were called the Caucasian race.

(8) I considered the horns, and behold, there came up among them another little horn, before whom there were three of the first horns plucked up by the roots: and behold, in this horn were eyes like the eyes of man, and a mouth speaking great things.

This little Horn is the Papacy of the Catholic Church; the same religious order Nimrod and Semiramis used, which they founded at the Tower of

Babel in Babylon. The name has changed, but the rituals and beliefs are basically the same. The Papacy under the consent of Rome established their own nation inside the overall boundary of Rome. Rome accepted their doctrine and called it Christianity around 369 AD. The Roman dictators granted the Catholic Church full power to make laws concerning all religious gathering and what or how the world believe. Tammaz, Semiramis son who died in a hunting accident was said to be the resurrected Christ and Semiramis became the Virgin Mary. The Cardinals were the same as Semiramis created them at the Tower of Babel. The catholic Church held this power for 1260 years; the Papacy was in control from 538 AD until 1798 AD; that is, until Napoleon sent his top General to Rome and arrested the Pope and threw him in prison.

(9) I beheld till the thrones were cast down, and the Ancient of days did sit, whose garment was white as snow, and the hair of his head like the pure wool: his throne was like the fiery flame, and his wheels as burning fire.

This verse carries us to the end of time and God sits on his throne issuing judgment on all his children. All kingdoms have come under the authority of our Heavenly Father.

(10) A fiery stream issued and came forth from before him: thousand, thousands ministered unto him, and ten thousand times ten thousand stood before him: the judgment was set, and the books were opened.

God is surrounded by all his children; the multitude of them is so great that they can't be counted. The books were opened, and each person is judged by what they did or didn't do while they were in the flesh body and how they conducted themselves during the 1000-year reign of Christ.

(11) I beheld then because of the voice of the great words which the horn spoke: I beheld even till

the beast was slain, and his body destroyed, and given to the burning flame. (pick up from page 116)

This is the end of Satan; God allows him to plead his case, but we already know what the verdict will be. God gave us this information in the book of Ezekiel.

Ezekiel Chapter 28:14-19

(14) Thou art the anointed cherub that covers; and I have set thee so: thou were upon the holy mountain of God; thou hast walked up and down in the midst of the stones of fire.

(15) Thou were perfect in thy ways from the day that thou were created, till iniquity was found in thee.

(16) By the multitude of thy merchandise they have filled the midst of thee with violence, and thou hast sinned: therefore, I will cast thee as profane out of the mountain of God: and I will destroy thee, O covering cherub, from the midst of the stones of fire.

(17) Thine heart was lifted up because of thy beauty, thou hast corrupted thy wisdom by reason of thy brightness: I will cast thee to the ground, I will lay thee before kings, that they may behold thee.

(18) Thou hast defiled thy sanctuaries by the multitude of thine iniquities, by the iniquity of thy traffick; therefore, will I bring forth a fire from the midst of thee, it shall devour thee, and I will bring thee to ashes upon the earth in the sight of all them that behold thee.

(19) All they that know thee among the people shall be astonished at thee: thou shalt be a terror, and never shalt thou be any more.

Satan is finished, no more to trouble God's children. Of course, this is just what God has prophesied to happen. It has not taken place yet. It will take place after the 'Great White Throne Judgment'. Now continuing on with the book of Daniel.

Daniel 7:12-27

(12) As concerning the rest of the beasts, they had their dominion taken away: yet their lives were prolonged for a season and time.

(13) I saw in the night visions, and behold, one like the Son of man came with the clouds of heaven, and came to the Ancient of days, and they brought him near before him.

(14) And there was given him dominion, and glory, and a kingdom, that all people, nations, and languages, should serve him: his dominion is an everlasting dominion, which shall not pass away, and his kingdom that which shall not be destroyed.

(15) I Daniel was grieved in my spirit in the midst of my body, and the visions of my head troubled me.

(16) I came near unto one of them that stood by and asked him the truth of all this. So, he told me, and made me know the interpretation of the things.

(17) These great beasts, which are four, are four kings, which shall arise out of the earth.

(18) But the saints of the most High shall take the kingdom, and possess the kingdom forever, even for ever and ever.

(19) Then I would know the truth of the fourth beast, which was diverse from all the others, exceeding dreadful, whose teeth were of iron, and his nails of brass, which devoured, brake in pieces, and stamped the residue with his feet.

(20) And of the ten horns that were in his head, and of the other which came up, and before whom three fell; even of that horn that had eyes, and a mouth that spoke very great things, whose look was stouter than his fellows.

(21) I beheld, and the same horn made war with the saints, and prevailed against them.

(22) Until the Ancient of days came, and judgment was given to the saints of the most High; and the time came that the saints possessed the kingdom.

(23) Thus, he said, the fourth beast shall be the fourth kingdom upon earth, which shall be diverse

from all kingdoms, and shall devour the whole earth, and shall tread it down, and break it in pieces.

(24) And the ten horns out of this kingdom are ten kings that shall arise: and another shall rise after them; and he shall be diverse from the first, and he shall subdue three kings.

(25) And he shall speak great words against the most High and shall wear out the saints of the most High and think to change times and laws: and they shall be given into his hand until a time and times and the dividing of time.

(26) But the judgment shall sit, and they shall take away his dominion, to consume and to destroy it unto the end.

(27) And the kingdom and dominion, and the greatness of the kingdom under the whole heaven, shall be given to the people of the saints of the most High, whose kingdom is an everlasting kingdom, and all dominions shall serve and obey him.

Chapter 7

Now, we'll leave the Old Testament and move into the New Testament years. We'll find God has made some changes; not really changes on his accord. But, because he gives all of his children freewill, to love him or not love him, some of the things God wanted for his children or hoped would happen have not come about. We can give Satan credit for this happening, or at least this is my belief.

I'm referring to the last chapters in the book of Ezekiel, Chapters 40 through 48. These chapter show the measurement of the Holy Temple and the size of it, how Christ would be worshipped, and how he would be perceived by his children on this physical earth; but there is one thing wrong, this the way the Temple of God would look if the people on earth accepted our Lord Christ the first time, he came to live with them. But as we all know, his children didn't accept him, but crucified him instead.

As Jesus said in the Gospel of Matthew, Chapter11:14

(14) And if ye will receive it, this is Elias, which was for to come.

But they didn't receive Jesus, so John was not Elijah. I threw this in because so many of us expected Elijah to return from the dead and announce the arrival of Christ; he could (nothing is impossible with God), but a lot of prophecies could be similar to John being Elijah. My thinking, my thinking; yours could be better.

And again: Matthew Chapter 17:10

(10) And his disciples asked him, saying, why then say the scribes that Elias must first come?

(11) And Jesus answered and said unto them, Elias truly shall first come, and restore all things.

(12) But I say unto you, that Elias is come already, and they knew him not, but have done unto him whatsoever they listed. Likewise, shall also the Son of man suffer of them.

And the Gospel of Mark declares in Mark 9:11-13.

(11) And they asked him, saying, why say the scribes that Elias must first come?

(12) And he answered and told them, Elias verily cometh first, and restoreth all things; and how it is written of the Son of man, that he must suffer many things, and be set at naught.

(13) But I say unto you, That Elias is indeed come, and they have done unto him whatsoever they listed, as it is written of him.

Do you still have doubts about my thinking? Perhaps, we can find some answers in the book of John. It is a bit different than the other gospels.

John 1:10

(10) He was in the world, and the world was made by him, and the world knew him not.

(11) He came unto his own, and his own received him not.

(12) But as many as received him, to them gave he power to become the sons of God, even to them that believe on his name:

(13) Which were born, not of blood, nor of the will of the flesh, nor of the will of man, but of God.

Are you thinking, 'if I had lived during those times,' and a lot of people did believe in him; they believed he had miraculous power and was maybe a prophet or a magician or something; anything, but God Almighty in a flesh body? Their minds couldn't make that leap; that the Creator of all things was walking around the earth he created in a flesh and blood body. Do you think you could have made this distinction and stood by him?

Christ chose 12 disciples and they traveled with him daily: eating and drinking with him. They watched as he performed miracle after miracle and Christ even told them he was God. Did they believe and accept him as such?

John 14:9

(9) Jesus saith unto him, Have I been so long time with you, and yet hast thou not known me, Philip? he that hath seen me hath seen the Father; and how sayest thou then, Shew us the Father?

What did Thomas say after Christ arose from the dead? We find this account in the book of John, chapter 20:24-29

(24) But Thomas, one of the twelve, called Didymus, was not with them when Jesus came.

(25) The other disciples therefore said unto him, we have seen the Lord. But he said unto them, Except I shall see in his hands the print of the nails and put

my finger into the print of the nails, and thrust my hand into his side, I will not believe.

(26) And after eight days again his disciples were within, and Thomas with them: then came Jesus, the doors being shut, and stood in the midst, and said, Peace be unto you.

(27) Then saith he to Thomas, reach hither thy finger, and behold my hands; and reach hither thy hand, and thrust it into my side: and be not faithless, but believing.

(28) And Thomas answered and said unto him, My Lord, and my God.

(29) Jesus saith unto him, Thomas, because thou hast seen me, thou hast believed: blessed are they that have not seen, and yet have believed.

Remember Thomas had walked with Jesus, had studied under Christ along with the other 11 and saw all the miracles; even the raising of Lazarus from the dead and he needed to see the risen Lord and feel his resurrected body before he would believe. And you think you would have been better than Thomas? I throw this question out to my readers because Christ will return again soon; how many of my fellow Christian will believe it's Christ returning if the exact words from the bible are not followed? Yeah? And you have not even seen the Lord yet? Do you know what he looks like? Can you tell him from the regular man on the street? What does the bible have to say on this subject?

1 John 4:1

(1) Beloved, believe not every spirit, but try the spirits whether they are of God: because many false prophets are gone out into the world.

How can you try every spirit? This is a good question; how do you try every spirit? Simple! Listen to what the person teaches or preaches and if it doesn't align with God's word, the Bible, it is a false prophet or spirit. This means you need to study your bible, so you know the plan of God and what has happened in the past. But be sure you have a correct bible, not some so called corrected works by man. Get yourself a KJV and a Strong's Concordance and find out what the bible tells you, not what some preacher or Sunday school teacher believes in. Remember, it's your very soul that's in danger of losing Heaven.

What did the Devil use to tempt Christ in the wilderness? Was it a beautiful woman? No! Was it fancy cars? No! How about money? Yes, in a way. The tempter used worldly things mostly. And his methods haven't changed. He'll used whatever he thinks you might care about more than God! Read how he tempted Christ and learn.

Matthew 4:1-10

(1) Then was Jesus led up of the Spirit into the wilderness to be tempted of the devil.

(2) And when he had fasted forty days and forty nights, he was afterward hungered.

(3) And when the tempter came to him, he said, if thou be the Son of God, command that these stones be made bread.

(4) But he answered and said, it is written, man shall not live by bread alone, but by every word that proceeded out of the mouth of God.

(5) Then the devil taketh him up into the holy city, and seats him on a pinnacle of the temple,

(6) And saith unto him, if thou be the Son of God, cast thyself down: for it is written, He shall give his angels charge concerning thee: and in their hands they shall bear thee up, lest at any time thou dash thy foot against a stone.

(7) Jesus said unto him, it is written again, thou shalt not tempt the Lord thy God.

(8) Again, the devil taketh him up into an exceeding high mountain, and shows him all the kingdoms of the world, and the glory of them.

(9) And saith unto him, all these things will I give thee, if thou wilt fall down and worship me.

(10) Then saith Jesus unto him, get thee hence, Satan: for it is written, thou shalt worship the Lord thy God, and him only shalt thou serve.

Do you understand what you have read? Love nothing more than God; not your children or any part of your family. Not your Country or your position in life. Nothing? Even as Abraham was willing to sacrifice his only son to obey the Father; even as Jesus, being God in the flesh, allowed himself to be crucified on a cross when he had done nothing wrong. Keep in mind, the flesh is weak and means nothing; your soul or spirit is everything in Gods eyes.

I hear what you are thinking. It is impossible to do all these things which God commands. And you are right; God knew this, so he gave us 10 more commandments after the first commandment which he gave to his children who have to live through this flesh age. We know them as the 10 commandments, and he said, if you obey these commandments, you shall live. So far, it's not recorded anywhere that this has happened. After six thousand years or so, not one person has been able to keep all these commands except Jesus. Some may have come close, but in trying to work your way into heaven, you are actually breaking the first Commandant. Don't believe me;

read the 1ˢᵗ commandment. What does it say? "Thou shall have no other gods before me." That's pretty plain, isn't it? So, in my thinking, if you want to work yourself into heaven, you have already broken the first commandment; that is, placing yourself before God.

Here is a list of the 10 commandments as found in Exodus Chapter 20 beginning with verse 3.

Exodus 20:3-17

(3) Thou shalt have no other gods before me.

(4) Thou shalt not make unto thee any graven image, or any likeness of anything that is in heaven above, or that is in the earth beneath, or that is in the water under the earth:

(5) Thou shalt not bow down thyself to them, nor serve them: for I, the LORD thy God am a jealous God, visiting the iniquity of the fathers upon the children unto the third and fourth generation of them that hate me.

(6) And shewing mercy unto thousands of them that love me and keep my commandments.

(7) Thou shalt not take the name of the LORD thy God in vain; for the LORD will not hold him guiltless that taketh his name in vain.

(8) Remember the sabbath day, to keep it holy.

(9) Six days shalt thou labor, and do all thy work:

(10) But the seventh day is the sabbath of the LORD thy God: in it thou shalt not do any work, thou, nor thy son, nor thy daughter, thy manservant, nor thy maidservant, nor thy cattle, nor thy stranger that is within thy gates:

(11) For in six days the LORD made heaven and earth, the sea, and all that in them is, and rested the seventh day: wherefore the LORD blessed the sabbath day and hallowed it.

(12) Honor thy father and thy mother: that thy days may be long upon the land which the LORD thy God giveth thee.

(13) Thou shalt not kill. (murder)

(14) Thou shalt not commit adultery.

(15) Thou shalt not steal.

(16) Thou shalt not bear false witness against thy neighbor.

(17) Thou shalt not covet thy neighbor's house, thou shalt not covet thy neighbor's wife, nor his manservant, nor his maidservant, nor his ox, nor his ass, nor any thing that is thy neighbor's.

There you have it; how many have you broken already? When I searched my life, I'm afraid I fell short and without the sacrifice of Christ, I would be doomed to the lake of fire. Notice, I didn't say 'Hell' because it doesn't exist yet. You are thinking, Christ mentioned 'Hell' in his parables quite often. Yes, that's the English translation from the Greek. What Christ said that the translator's mis-translated 'Hell' is the Greek work, 'Gehenna', which was a garbage pit outside of Jerusalem. It was a place where dead animals and human bodies were tossed if the dead one had nobody to care enough about them to provide a decent burial. The authorities kept a fire burning there at all times so the smell of rotting flesh wouldn't be so bad. The place had rats and any kind of vermin which is attracted to rotten flesh scurrying about to eat what they could. Rightly so, Christ could use this imagery to describe the holding place unsaved spirits would be kept until the 'Great White Throne Judgment' was held.

In the Old Testament, the word translated 'Hell' is Shoal and all it means is a holding place of the spirits, which fits in nicely with the New Testament. All Spirits, good of bad are waiting for the final judgment by God before anything permanent can happen to them. So, until that day, you still have a chance to make eternal life with Christ. God knows all of the ignorant teachings being taught his children and he will not condemn anyone without them knowing the truth of who he is and what he stands for; than you can choose who you want to be with God or Satan. I've already told you where Satan will end up, so be very careful in your choses.

What did Christ have to say about the Old Testament law? (ten commandments)

Matthew 5:17-18

(17) Think not that I am come to destroy the law, or the prophets: I am not come to destroy, but to fulfil.

(18) For verily I say unto you, till heaven and earth pass, one jot or one tittle shall in no wise pass from the law, till all be fulfilled.

Now you know the same law the people lived under thousands of years age are still the same law we live under and will be the same law all will live under until Judgment Day.

God is the same today as he was yesterday and will be tomorrow.

John 1:29

(29) The next day John sees Jesus coming unto him, and saith, Behold the Lamb of God, which taketh away the sin of the world.

How can one man take away the sin of the world? Remember way back in the 'Garden of Eden' when God told Adam not to have anything to do with the 'Tree of knowledge of good and evil', because if he did, he would die? Well Adam screwed up and both Adam and Eve partook of that Tree, which was in reality, Lucifer or Satan or the Devil; well, that was the day they died. No not the way most people think; the physical body didn't die, but the spirit of one of God's children that God had placed in the flesh body of Adam died that day. Only God didn't carry out the death sentence at that time, but when the flesh man, Adam, died and his spirit was released, God placed the spirit of Adam in a holding cell. This cell is where the rich man in the story parable of 'Lazarus and the rich man' was located. The cell is across a wide gulf from Heaven where God lives. Adam's spirit is in Heaven alright, but not the good part of Heaven. Furthermore, all souls are placed there when the flesh plays out and dies, unless you are one of God's elect.

God will not look upon sin and the only way for all of God's children who went astray and sinned could be reconciled back to our Heavenly Father, would have to be made by a blood sacrifice. Why a blood sacrifice? A blood sacrifice has to be done because the

life of all physical creatures is in the blood. And the
only sacrifice God would accept is if the one making
the sacrifice cared more for the one being sacrificed
than their own life. Abraham was willing to make this
kind of sacrifice when God told him to kill his only
child and sacrifice him to God. Abraham was willing to
obey God's command; but God stopped the sacrifice
from being made this way. He provided a Ram for
Abraham to use for the sacrifice. In the eons of time,
God would make this sacrifice himself in the flesh
man, Jesus the Christ. Without this sacrifice, at least a
third of God's children would die of their sins. Maybe
more, we are told in the Bible, a third of God's
children followed Satan in the attempted revolt, but
what about the ones who didn't do anything? You
know the ones standing on the sidelines watching.
The ones who didn't care who won the battle; they
would follow the winner. How many were of this class.
The bible doesn't tell us, but judging by the way
people still act, I'd say at least another third. What do
you think; I'm just guessing. Anyway, you look at the
situation, a lot of souls were at stake. Sure, I know

God could have wiped the whole mess away and started anew, but would you kill a third or more of your children when they did wrong, even if you and your wife could still produce more children? No! I didn't think so, and God didn't think so either. The Bible tells us, God destroyed everything except his children and started over.

Jeremiah 4:23-28

(23) I beheld the earth, and, lo, it was without form, and void; and the heavens, and they had no light.

(24) I beheld the mountains, and, lo, they trembled, and all the hills moved lightly.

(25) I beheld, and, lo, there was no man, and all the birds of the heavens were fled.

(26) I beheld, and, lo, the fruitful place was a wilderness, and all the cities thereof were broken down at the presence of the LORD, and by his fierce anger.

(27) For thus hath the LORD said, the whole land shall be desolate; yet will I not make a full end.

(28) For this shall the earth mourn, and the heavens above be black: because I have spoken it, I have purposed it, and will not repent, neither will I turn back from it.

When the verse above says, 'I beheld', it means God is looking at what he has just destroyed.

This destruction by God happened after the revolt caused by Lucifer was put down. At this time God had two choses, either kill a third or more of his children who he loves or destroy the universe and create a new earth and a new heaven. He chose to destroy everything except his children and start over.

Now we have the 1st verse of Genesis, chapter one. "In the beginning, God created the Heaven and the Earth." This is the beginning of the flesh age.

Chapter 8

When was Jesus born? Yes, I know we celebrate Jesus' birthday on Christmas Day; but is this his real birthday? Is there anyway to prove what day Jesus was born on? YES! Yes, to all the questions I just asked. It's going to take a little digging through the bible to find out but it's there. I'm going to should you how to do it the exact day Jesus was born, that is, within a day or two, anyway.

When we start searching the scriptures for Jesus' birthday, we'll have to start with John the Baptist. Why start with John the Baptist, you might ask? Well, the answer is simple because the bible lets us know Christ was born 6 months after the birth of John. So, if we can determine John's date of birth, all we have to do is add 6 months. So, first, let's try to find John's date of birth.

Luke 1:5

(5) There was in the days of Herod, the king of Judaea, a certain priest named Zacharias, of the course of Abia: and his wife was of the daughters of Aaron, and her name was Elisabeth.

(6) And they were both righteous before God, walking in all the commandments and ordinances of the Lord blameless.

(7) And they had no child, because that Elisabeth was barren, and they both were now well stricken in years.

(8) And it came to pass, that while he executed the priest's office before God in the order of his course,

(9) According to the custom of the priest's office, his lot was to burn incense when he went into the temple of the Lord.

(10) And the whole multitude of the people were praying without at the time of incense.

(11) And there appeared unto him an angel of the Lord standing on the right side of the altar of incense.

(12) And when Zacharias saw him, he was troubled, and fear fell upon him.

(13) But the angel said unto him, Fear not, Zacharias: for thy prayer is heard; and thy wife Elisabeth shall bear thee a son, and thou shalt call his name John.

Ok. Here in the book of Luke an Angel, Gabriel, informs Zacharias he is going to have a child. Where is Zacharias working or what is he doing at the time the Angel Gabriel appears to him? Zacharias is a Levite, and he is doing his duty in the temple of the Lord. What else do we know about John? Luke informs us Zacharias is a priest of the course of Abia. What do we know about the course of Abia or for that matter about any of the courses performed in the temple of Lord in those days? Nothing or very little at the most.

1 Chronicles 24:1-19

(1) Now these are the divisions of the sons of Aaron. The sons of Aaron; Nadab, and Abihu, Eleazar, and Ithamar.

(2) But Nadab and Abihu died before their father, and had no children: therefore, Eleazar and Ithamar executed the priest's office.

(3) And David distributed them, both Zadok of the sons of Eleazar, and Ahimelech of the sons of Ithamar, according to their offices in their service.

(4) And there were more chief men found of the sons of Eleazar than of the sons of Ithamar; and thus, were they divided. Among the sons of Eleazar there were sixteen chief men of the house of their fathers, and eight among the sons of Ithamar according to the house of their fathers.

(5) Thus, were they divided by lot, one sort with another; for the governors of the sanctuary, and governors of the house of God, were of the sons of Eleazar, and of the sons of Ithamar.

(6) And Shemaiah the son of Nethaneel the scribe, one of the Levites, wrote them before the king, and the princes, and Zadok the priest, and Ahimelech

the son of Abiathar, and before the chief of the fathers of the priests and Levites: one principal household being taken for Eleazar, and one taken for Ithamar.

(7) Now the first lot came forth to Jehoiarib, the second to Jedaiah,

(8) The third to Harim, the fourth to Seorim,

(9) The fifth to Malchijah, the sixth to Mijamin,

(10) The seventh to Hakkoz, the eighth to Abijah,

(11) The ninth to Jeshua, the tenth to Shecaniah,

(12) The eleventh to Eliashib, the twelfth to Jakim,

(13) The thirteenth to Huppah, the fourteenth to Jeshebeab,

(14) The fifteenth to Bilgah, the sixteenth to Immer,

15The seventeenth to Hezir, the eighteenth to Aphses,

16The nineteenth to Pethahiah, the twentieth to Jehezekel,

17The one and twentieth to Jachin, the two and twentieth to Gamul,

18The three and twentieth to Delaiah, the four and twentieth to Maaziah.

19These were the orderings of them in their service to come into the house of the LORD, according to their manner, under Aaron their father, as the LORD God of Israel had commanded him.

You'll see by reading this list of courses, there are 24 courses for the year which begins on the Spring Equinox. These courses run one week each and each starts on a sabbath.

Jewish:	Western:
Tebeth 29 days.	December 7days
Sebat 30 days	January 31days
Adar 29 days	February 29 days

NISAN 30 days	MARCH 31 days
ZIF 29 days	APRIL 30 days
SIVAN 30 days	MAY 31 days
THAMMUZ 29 days	JUNE 30 days
AB 30 days	JULY 31 days
ELUL 29 days	AUGUST 31 days
ETHANIM 15 days	SEPTEMBER 29 days
280 total days	280 total days

========== ==========

280 days = 40 weeks - forty sevens, the perfect period of human gestation [7x5x8=280].

The Component Numbers of 280 are highly significant in this connection.

7 denotes Spiritual Perfection.

5 denotes Divine Grace.

8 denotes Resurrection, Regeneration, etc. (Appendix 10).

1st TEBETH = 25th December (5 B.C.)

15th ETHANIM = 29th September (4 B.C.).

From 1st TEBETH to 15th ETHANIM (inclusive) = 280 days.

From 25th DECEMBER (5 B.C.) to 29th
SEPTEMBER (4 B.C.) = 280 days.

The next text is from Appendix 179, by E.W.
Bullinger's Companion Bible: Pages 147-162

1. It thus appears without the shadow of a
doubt that the day assigned to the Birth of the Lord,
videlicet: December 25, was the day on which He was
"begotten of the Holy Ghost", that is to say, by
pneuma hagion = divine power (Matthew 1:18, 20
marg.), and His birth took place on the 15th of
Ethanim, September 29, in the year following, thus
making beautifully clear the meaning of John
1:14,"The Word became flesh" (Matthew 1:18,20) on
1st Tebeth or December 25 (5 B.C.), "and tabernacled
(Greek eskenosen) with us", on 15th of Ethanim or
September 29 (4 B.C.).

The 15th of Ethanim (or Tisri) was the first day
of the Feast of Tabernacles. The Circumcision
therefore took place on the eighth day of the Feast =
22nd Ethanim = October 6-7 (Leviticus 23:33-43). So

that these two momentous events fall into their proper place and order, and the real reason is made clear why the 25th of December is associated with our Lord and was set apart by the Apostolic Church to commemorate the stupendous event of the "Word becoming flesh" – and not, as we have for so long been led to suppose the commemoration of a pagan festival.

2. An overwhelmingly strong argument in favor of the correctness of this view lies in the fact that the date of "the Festival of Michael and All Angels" has been from very early times the 29th day of September, on Gentile (Western) reckoning.

But "the Church" even then had lost sight of the reason why this date rather than any other in the Calendar should be so indissolubly associated with the great Angelic Festival.

The following expresses the almost universal knowledge or rather want of knowledge of "Christendom" on the subject: "We pass on now to consider, in the third place, the commemoration of September 29, the festival of Michaelmas, par excellence. It does not appear at all certain what was the original special idea of the commemoration of this day" (Smith Dictionary of Chr. Antiqq. (1893), volume ii, page 1177 (A)).

A reference, however, to the Table and statements above, make the "original special idea" why the Festival of "Michael and All Angels" is held on September 29 abundantly clear. Our Lord was born on that day, the first day of the "Feast of Tabernacle" (Leviticus 23:39). This was on the fifteenth day of the seventh Jewish month called Tisri, or Ethanim (Appendix 51. 5), corresponding to our September 29 (of the year 4 B.C.). The "Begetting" (genesis) Day of the Lord was announced by the Angel Gabriel. See notes on Daniel 8:16, and Luke 1:19.

The "Birth" Day, by "(the) Angel of the Lord", unnamed in either Matthew and Luke.

That this Angelic Being was "Michael the Archangel" (of Jude 9), and "Mika'el hassar haggadol-"Michael the Great Prince"-of Daniel 12:1, seems clear for the following reason: If, "when again (yet future) He bringeth the First-begotten into the world, He saith, let all the Angels of God worship Him" (Hebrews 1:6; quoting Psalm 97:6)-then this must include the great Archangel Michael himself. By parity of reasoning, on

the First "bringing" into the world of the only begotten Son, the Archangel must have been present. And the tremendous announcement to the shepherds, that the Prince of Peace (Isaiah 9:6) was on earth in the person of the Babe of Bethlehem, must therefore have been made by the same head of the heavenly host (Luke 2:9-14). In mundane affairs, announcement of supremist importance (of Kings, etc.) are invariably conveyed through the most exalted personage in the realm. The point need not be labored.

3. The fact of the Birth of our Lord having been revealed to the shepherds by the Archangel Michael on the 15th of Tisri (or Ethtanim), corresponding to September 29, 4 B.C.-the first day of the Feast of Tabernacles-must have been known to believers in the Apostolic Age. But "the mystery of iniquity" which was "already working" in Paul's day

(2 Thessalonians 2:7) quickly enshrouded this and the other great fact of the Jewish month Tebeth (corresponding to December 25, 5 B.C.)-as well as other connected with His sojourn on earth,4-in a rising mist of obscurity in which they have ever since been lost.

The earliest allusion to December 25 (modern reckoning) as the date for the Nativity is found in the Stromata of Clement of Alexandria, about the beginning of the third century A.D. (See note 3).5

That "Christmas" was a pagan festival long before the time of our Lord is beyond doubt. In Egypt Horus (or Hippocrates 6), the son of Isis (Queen of Heaven), was born about the time of the winter solstice.7 By the time of the early part of the fourth century A.D., the real reason for observing Christmas as the date for the miraculous "begetting" of Matthew 1:18 and "the Word becoming flesh" of John 1:14 had been lost sight of. The policy of Constantine, and his Edict of Milan, by establishing universal freedom of religion furthered this. When many of the followers of the old pagan systems-the vast majority of the empire, it must be remembered- adopted the Christian religion as a cult, which Constantine had made fashionable, and the "Church" became the Church of the Roman Empire, they brought in with them, among a number of other things emanating from Egypt and Babylon, the various Festival Days of the old "religious". Thus "Christmas Day," the birthday of the Egyptian Horus (Osiris), became gradually substituted for the real Natalis Domini of our blessed Savior, videlicet: September 29, or Michaelmas Day.

4. If, however, we realize that the center of gravity, so to speak, of what we call the Incarnation is the Incarnation itself- the wondrous fact of the Divine "begetting", when "the Word became flesh" (see Matthew 1:18 and John 1:14) - and that this is to be associated with December 25 instead of March - as for 1,600 years Christendom has been led to believe- then "Christmas" will be seen in quite another light, and many who have hitherto been troubled with scruples concerning the day being, as they have been taught, the anniversary of a Pagan festival, will be enabled to worship on that Day without alloy of doubt,

as the time when the stupendous miracle which is the foundation stone of the Christian faith, came to pass.

The "Annunciation" by the Angel Gabriel marked the genesis of Matthew 1:18, and the first words of John 1:14.

The announcement to the shepherds by the Archangel Michael marked the Birth of our Lord. John 1:14 is read as though "the Word became flesh (Revised Version), and dwelt among us", were one and the same thing where - as they are two clauses.

The paragraph should read thus: "And the Word became flesh; (Greek ho logos sarx egeneto.) And tabernacled with (or among) us." (Greek kai eskenosen en hemin).

The word tabernacled here (preserved in Revised Version marg.) receives beautiful significance from the knowledge that "the Lord of Glory" was "found in fashion as a man", and thus tabernacling in human flesh. And in turn it shows in equally beautiful significance that our Lord was born on the first day of the great Jewish Feast of Tabernacles, videlicet: the

15th of Tisri, corresponding to September 29, 4 B.C. (modern reckoning).

The circumcision of our Lord took place therefore on the eighth day, the last day of the Feast, the "Great Day of the Feast" of John 7:37 ("Tabernacles" had eight days. The Feast of Unleavened Bread had seven days, and Pentecost one. See Leviticus 23).

5. The main arguments against the Nativity having taken place in December may be set forth very simply:

(i) The extreme improbability, amounting almost to impossibility, that Mary, under such circumstances, could have undertaken a journey of about 70 miles (as the crow flies), through a hill district averaging some 3,000 feet above sea - level, in the depth of winter: (ii) Shepherds and their flocks would not be found "abiding" (Greek agrauleo) in the open fields at night in December (Tebeth), for the paramount reason that there would be no pasturage at that time. It was the custom then (as now) to withdraw the flocks during the month Marchesvan

(October-November)8 from the open districts and house them for the winter.

(iii) The Roman authorities in imposing such a "census taking" for the hated and unpopular "foreign" tax would not have enforced the imperial decree (Luke 2:1) at the most inconvenient and inclement season of the year, by compelling the people to enroll themselves at their respective "cities" in December. In such a case they would naturally choose the "line" of least resistance" and select a time of year that would cause least friction, and interference with the habits and pursuits of the Jewish people. This would be in the autumn, when the agricultural round of the year was complete, and the people generally more or less at liberty to take advantage, as we know many did, of the opportunity of "going up" to Jerusalem for the "Feast of Tabernacles" (compare John 7:8-10, etc.), the crowning Feast of the Jewish year.

To take advantage of such a time would be to the Romans the simplest and most natural policy, whereas to attempt to enforce the Edict of Registration for the purposes of Imperial taxation in the depth of winter, -when travelling for such a purpose would have been deeply resented, and perhaps have brought about a revolt, -would never have been attempted by such an astute ruler as Augustus.

6. With regard to the other two "Quarter Days", June 24, March 25, these are both associated with the miraculous (Luke 1:7) "conception" and the birth of the Forerunner, as December 25 and September 29 are with our Lord's miraculous "Begetting" and Birth; and are therefore connected with "the Course of Abiah."

III."THE COURSE OF ABIA" (Luke 1:5).

This was the eighth of the priestly courses of ministration in the Temple (1Chronicles 24:10), and occurred, as did the others, twice in the year.

The "Courses "were changed every week, beginning each with a Sabbath. The reckoning commenced on the 22nd day of Tisri or Ethanim (Appendix 51. 5).

This was the eighth and last day of the Feast of Tabernacles = the "Great Day of the Feast" (John 7:37) and was a Sabbath (Leviticus 23:39).

The first course fell by lot to Jehoiarib, and the eighth to Abia or Abijah (1Chronicles 24:10).

Bearing in mind that all the courses served together at the three Great Feasts, the dates for the two yearly "ministrations" of Abiah will be seen to fall as follows: The first 9 ministration was from 12-18 Chisleu = December 6-12. The second ministration was from 12-18 Sivan = June 13-19.

The announcement therefore to Zacharias in the Temple as to the conception of John the Baptist took place between 12-18 SIVAN (June 13-19), in the year 5 B.C.

After finishing his "ministration", the aged priest "departed to his own house" (Luke 1:23), which was in a city in "the hill country" of Juda (verse 39).

The day following the end of the "Course of Abia" being a Sabbath (Sivan 19), he would not be able to leave Jerusalem before the 20th.

The thirty miles journey would probably occupy, for an old man, a couple of days at least. He would therefore arrive at his house on the 21st or 22nd. This

leaves ample time for the miraculous "conception" of Elizabeth to take place on or about 23rd of SIVAN 11 - which would correspond to June 23-24 of that year.

The fact of the conception and its date would necessarily be known at the time and afterwards, and hence the 23rd SIVAN would henceforth be associated with the conception of John Baptist as the 1st TEBETH would be with that of our Lord.

But the same influences that speedily obscured and presently obliterated the real dates of our Lord's "Begetting" and Birth, were also at work with regard to those of the Forerunner, and with the same results. As soon as the true Birthday of Christ had been shifted from its proper date, videlicet: the 15th of Tisri (September 29), and a Festival Day from the Pagan Calendars substituted for it (videlicet: December 25), then everything else had to be altered too.

Hence "Lady Day" in association with March 25 (new style) became necessarily connected with the Annunciation. And June 24 made its appearance, as it still is in our Calendar, as the date of "the Nativity of John the Baptist", instead of, as it really is, the date of his miraculous conception.

The Four "Quarter Days" may therefore be set forth thus: first in the chronological order of the events with which they are associated, videlicet:

The conception of John Baptist

on or about 23rd SIVAN = June 24

in the year 5 B.C.

The Genesis (Begetting) of our Lord

on or about 1st TEBETH = December 25

in the year 5 B.C.

The birth of John Baptist on or about 4th-7th NISAN

= March 25-28

in the year 4

B.C.

The birth of our Lord on or about 15th TISRI =

September 29

in the year 4

B.C.

 or placing the two sets together naturally: -

{The conception of John 23rd SIVAN = June 23-24 in the year 5

B.C.

{The birth of John 7th NISAN = March 28-29 in the year 4

B.C.

{The Miraculous

"Begetting"

1st TEBETH = December

25

in the year 5

B.C.

{The NATIVITY 15th TISRI = September 29 in the year 4

B.C.

NOTES

(1) ZUMPT fixes Quirinus' (Cyrenius') First Governorship as 4 B.C. to 1 B.C. Justin Martyr thrice says that our Lord was born under Quirinus (Apol. 1. XXXIV, page 37; XLVI, page 46; Dial. LXXVIII, page 195. Clarks edition).

(2) According to some, Augustus died August 19, A.D. 14. Therefore, if Tiberius' coregnancy was for two years before Augustus' death his first year was 765 A.U.C. = 12 A.D. His fifteenth year consequently was A.U.C. 779 = 26 A.D. = 4030 A.M. and A.C. 30, for our Lord was thirty years of age when He began His Ministry (Luke 3:23). Clement of Alexandria gives the years of Augustus' reign as being 43-46, according to different reckonings in his day.

(3) According to Clement of Alexandria (compare A.D. 190-220) "Our Lord was born in the twenty-eighth year when first the census was ordered

to be taken in the reign of Augustus" (Stromata, Book i, see Clark's edition i. pages 444-445).

If that is correct, and it is true that a Census was taken every fourteen years, then the next would fall in A.D. 10, and the succeeding one would have been due A.D. 24.

(4) Notably the day of the crucifixion, etc. (see Appendix 156 and Appendix 165).

(5) His statements are, however, very vague, and he mentions several dates

claimed by others as correct.

(6) Osiris reincarnated.

(7) See Wilkinson's Ancient Egyptians, Volume III, page 79 (Birch's edition).

(8) It is true that the Lebanon shepherds are in the habit of keeping their flocks alive during the winter months, by cutting down branches of trees in the forests in that district, to feed the sheep on the leaves and twigs, when in autumn the pastures are dried up, and in winter, when snow covers the ground (compare

Land and Book, page 204), but there is no evidence that the Bethlehem district was afforested in the manner.

(9) Reckoning of course from Ethanim or Tisri - the First month of the civil year.

The sacred year was six month later and began on 1st Nisan.

(10) The "city" is not named (possibly Juttah, some 30 miles to the south of Jerusalem).

(11) The conception of John Baptist was, in view of Luke 1:7, as miraculous as that of Isaac; but it is not necessary to insist upon the complete period of forty sevens in the case of Elizabeth. Therefore, the birth of the Forerunner may have been three or four days short of the full two hundred and eighty days, - as indicated in the above table.

Reference: Companion Bible Appendix 179 by E. W. Bullinger.

Whether you want to accept Jesus being born on our September the 29 is up to you. All I have done is give you the facts the best I can; what you do with the fact is up to you. If you back up the calendar 9 months, it gives December as the month of conception and the date would be most likely the 25. Since life of a child begins at conception, Jesus life in the womb begins near our Christmas day; so, you can still celebrate Christ at Christmas if you care to look at the life of Jesus being here at this time.

But does it really make any difference? In my mind, the way he lived and his death and why he died is what's important.

Chapter 9

(8) I am Alpha and Omega, the beginning, and the ending, saith the Lord, which is, and which was, and which is to come, the Almighty.

John, around 95 A.D. has been imprisoned on the Isle of Patmos for believing in Christ. It is here where he receives this message of the Revelation of Jesus Christ.

The words, Alpha is the Greek for beginning and the word Omega is the Greek for ending. As we learned in the gospel of John, chapter one, verse one thru 3

(1) In the beginning was the Word, and the Word was with God, and the Word was God.

(2) The same was in the beginning with God.

(3) All things were made by him; and without him was not anything made that was made.

I know we looked at this earlier in our study, but I wanted to refresh your mind as to the full nature of Christ. He is God and can assume any form or shape he decides to use to make his point or deliver the message to whomever he chooses. As in the case of Balaam as told in the book of Numbers, when he had the jackass speak to Balaam to get his message across. You see, Balaam, although a servant of God, like money and things of the world. God used extraordinary methods to convince Balaam to do the Lord's work and forget all else.

So now, we are getting to the end of our study of the bible; all that left is understanding the future that God will bring about at the right time. I hope you are not one of those who think this age or world is rolling along without some guidance from our Lord. The happenings in this age are similar to a physical parent letting a child get hurt so he can learn a timely lesson to sustain the child in the future.

For instance, In the old days when I was a child, we used a wood cook stove to prepare our meals. Most stoves of that time period were made of cast iron and became very hot when being used to cook a meal. Children playing in the house or doing chores were told to be careful of the hot cooking stove because if they touched it, they would get burn and feel a lot of pain. A careless child might touch the hot stove accidently or cautiously put their finger to the hot metal, but never again because they will always remember burning their hand or finger.

Our Heavenly father allows us, his children, to experience the same thing in life. He has given us rules to live by and enough sense to avoid danger, but if we ignorant his teachings, we'll experience a lot of pain.

This warning having been given, let's take a look at what our God has in store for us in the future.

The future events are what the book of Revelation is all about; we just need to study it and learn what it takes to stay in focus and safe.

The message John Is to receive is for the seven churches scattered in what we know as Asia-Minor now days. These churches are basically scattered on the westside of the modern-day country of Turkey. But the locations of these churches are not important in my way of thinking. I believe the message Christ sent to each church is important for them as well as us to learn what pleases God/Christ. So, let's look at each church and with God's help, grasp the truth.

While we are studying, always keep in mind, the Catholic Church had sole control of the bible and what was written in it for 1260 years; that is from 538 A.D. until 1798 A.D. It will never be known in our flesh life if the Papacy changed any of the scriptures or not. But what it is; is what it is.

After the Angel informs John who he is and why he has come, the angel delivers the message for John to write down.

Revelation 1:1,

(1) The Revelation of Jesus Christ, which God gave unto him, to shew unto his servant's things which must shortly come to pass; and he sent and signified it by his angel unto his servant John:

(2) Who bare record of the word of God, and of the testimony of Jesus Christ, and of all things that he saw.

(3) Blessed is he that reads, and they that hear the words of this prophecy, and keep those things which are written therein: for the time is at hand.

(4) John to the seven churches which are in Asia: Grace be unto you, and peace, from him which is, and which was, and which is to come; and from the seven Spirits which are before his throne.

(5) And from Jesus Christ, who is the faithful witness, and the first begotten of the dead, and the prince of the kings of the earth. Unto him that loved us, and washed us from our sins in his own blood,

(6) And hath made us kings and priests unto God and his Father; to him be glory and dominion for ever and ever. Amen.

(7) Behold, he cometh with clouds; and every eye shall see him, and they also which pierced him: and all kindreds of the earth shall wail because of him. Even so, Amen.

(8) I am Alpha and Omega, the beginning, and the ending, saith the Lord, which is, and which was, and which is to come, the Almighty

The Angel has described to John who he is and why he has come. He has a message from our Lord and Savior, Jesus Christ, who describes himself as being the first begotten of the dead, a faithful witness, and as the prince of the kings of the earth. He tells John he is alive now, and he lived before he died on the cross, and he is the one predicted to come in the future and from the seven Spirits who resides before his throne. The prediction of his coming is given in the book of Deuteronomy, chapter 18, verses 15 and 18.

(15) The LORD thy God will raise up unto thee a Prophet from the midst of thee, of thy brethren, like unto me; unto him ye shall hearken.

(18) I will raise them up a Prophet from among their brethren, like unto thee, and will put my words

in his mouth; and he shall speak unto them all that I shall command him.

Next, John tells his readers who he is and where he is being held.

(9) I John, who also am your brother, and companion in tribulation, and in the kingdom and patience of Jesus Christ, was in the isle that is called Patmos, for the word of God, and for the testimony of Jesus Christ.

John tells us he was in the Spirit on the Lords Day when he heard a voice behind him as of a trumpet.

Revelation 1:11

(11) Saying, I am Alpha and Omega, the first and the last: and, what thou see, write in a book, and send it unto the seven churches which are in Asia; unto Ephesus, and unto Smyrna, and unto Pergamos, and unto Thyatira, and unto Sardis, and unto Philadelphia, and unto Laodicea.

John receives his instruction; he knows what his orders are. Because the voice who spoke to him is so commanding, John turns to see who or where this voice originates. John knows it's not coming from the Angel who stands before him and has been speaking to him. When John turns, he sees 7 golden candlesticks and among them a person like the Son of man and he is clothed head to foot.

Revelation 1:13-17

(13) And in the midst of the seven candlesticks one like unto the Son of man, clothed with a garment down to the foot, and girt about the paps with a golden girdle.

(14) His head and his hairs were white like wool, as white as snow; and his eyes were as a flame of fire.

(15) And his feet like unto fine brass, as if they burned in a furnace, and his voice as the sound of many waters.

(16) And he had in his right hand seven stars: and out of his mouth went a sharp two-edged sword: and his countenance was as the sun shineth in his strength.

(17) And when I saw him, I fell at his feet as dead. And he laid his right hand upon me, saying unto me, Fear not; I am the first and the last:

I know if I saw a figure such as John witnessed, I would be scared stiff. So, whether John was frightened or not, he listened to the message he was given. I think John recognized the figure as being our Lord, Jesus the Christ.

(18) I am he that lived, and was dead; and behold, I am alive for evermore, amen; and have the keys of hell and of death.

(19) Write the things which thou hast seen, and the things which are, and the things which shall be hereafter.

(20) The mystery of the seven stars which thou sawest in my right hand, and the seven golden candlesticks. The seven stars are the angels of the seven churches: and the seven candlesticks which thou sawest are the seven churches.

After describing to John, the meaning of the 7 golden candlesticks and the 7 stars, he gives John the message he wants delivered to these churches. Let me remind you, the churches in the 1st century area would not look like the churches of today. The message to the church at Ephesus is stated:

Revelation 2:1-7

(1) Unto the angel of the church of Ephesus write, these things saith he that holds the seven stars in his right hand, who walketh in the midst of the seven golden candlesticks.

(2) I know thy works, and thy labor, and thy patience, and how thou canst not bear them which are evil: and thou hast tried them which say they are apostles, and are not, and hast found them liars:

(3) And hast borne, and hast patience, and for my name's sake hast labored, and hast not fainted.

(4) Nevertheless, I have somewhat against thee because thou hast left thy first love.

(5) Remember therefore from whence thou art fallen, and repent, and do the first works; or else I will come unto thee quickly, and will remove thy candlestick out of his place, except thou repent.

(6) But this thou hast, that thou hate the deeds of the Nicolaitans, which I also hate.

(7) He that hath an ear, let him hear what the Spirit saith unto the churches; To him that overcomes will I give to eat of the tree of life, which is in the midst of the paradise of God.

What did Christ say was wrong with the Church at Ephesus? They had lost their first love; your first love is always the love of our Heavenly Father. Meaning this church had started putting other things, like material gifts and personal prestige ahead of showing the love of Christ to all. Maybe, they spent more time raising money for some pet project than in being faithful to God. It could have been several different things; anything you love more than fellowship with our Lord is wrong. Remember the 1st Commandment? The love of God comes first.

(8) And unto the angel of the church in Smyrna write, these things saith the first and the last, which was dead, and is alive.

(9) I know thy works, and tribulation, and poverty, (but thou art rich) and I know the blasphemy of them which say they are Jews, and are not, but are the synagogue of Satan.

(10) Fear none of those things which thou shalt suffer, behold, the devil shall cast some of you into prison, that ye may be tried; and ye shall have tribulation ten days: be thou faithful unto death, and I will give thee a crown of life

(11) He that hath an ear, let him hear what the Spirit saith unto the churches; He that overcomes shall not be hurt of the second death.

The Smyrna church probably didn't have a lot of capital to work with and felt they were being looked down on by the other churches or maybe the Christian community as a whole; but Christ said they were rich. They recognized who the people were who were Kenites. You do remember the Kenites, children of Cain, whom God placed a Mark on? Well, they were troublemakers in the synagogue during Jesus' life in the flesh and they are still troublemakers at the Smyrna Church and, guess what, they are still around our churches today. They look like everybody else, so how can you tell them from God's people? Christ said you'll know them by their works. Example: how many churches did Christ start through Paul? Did I understand you to say 'one'? That's right, only one church; how many do we have in this 21st Century? 100; maybe more; maybe less. Why? Division: who likes to mess up God's plan? If you commented, Satan, you could go to the head of the class. As Paul stated in his letter to the Corinthians,

1 Corinthians 1:12

(12) Now this I say, that every one of you saith, I am of Paul; and I of Apollos; and I of Cephas; and I of Christ.

1 Corinthians 3:4

(4) or while one saith, I am of Paul; and another, I am of Apollos; are ye not carnal?

(5) Who then is Paul, and who is Apollos, but ministers by whom ye believed, even as the Lord gave to every man?

(6) I have planted, Apollos watered; but God gave the increase.

1 Corinthians 3:22

(22) Whether Paul, or Apollos, or Cephas, or the world, or life, or death, or things present, or things to come; all are yours.

You can see, God has only one church, and all the divisions we see today are caused by people thinking their beliefs are more important than God's word.

Revelation 2:12 -17

(12) And to the angel of the church in Pergamos write; These things saith he which hath the sharp sword with two edges.

(13) I know thy works, and where thou dwellest, even where Satan's seat is and thou hold fast my name, and hast not denied my faith, even in those days wherein Antipas was my faithful martyr, who was slain among you, where Satan dwelleth.

(14) But I have a few things against thee because thou hast there them that hold the doctrine of Balaam, who taught Balac to cast a stumbling block before the children of Israel, to eat things sacrificed unto idols, and to commit fornication.

(15) So hast thou also them that hold the doctrine of the Nicolaitans, which thing I hate.

(16) Repent; or else I will come unto thee quickly and will fight against them with the sword of my mouth.

(17) He that hath an ear, let him hear what the Spirit saith unto the churches; To him that overcomes will I give to eat of the hidden manna, and will give him a white stone, and in the stone a new name written, which no man knows saving he that received it.

What is the sword with two edges? In our 1st chapter in the book of revelation, we see a person with a two-edged sword coming out his mouth. We know this is Christ but what does the sword with two edges coming out his mouth mean? We find our answer in the book of Hebrews

Hebrews 4:12

(12) For the word of God is quick, and powerful, and sharper than any two-edged sword, piercing even to the dividing asunder of soul and spirit, and of the joints and marrow, and is a discerner of the thoughts and intents of the heart. Christ hates the doctrine of the Nicolaitans, so what is this doctrine? Briefly,

Nicolaitanism Today:

In the main, these papers defined Nicolaitanism as the belief and practice of hierarchical government, the scapegoat for all the church's problems, with an emphasis on tithing and using a paid ministry. This definition derives from the meaning of the word Nicolaos in Greek: "conqueror of the people" (Balaam in Hebrew has a similar meaning). The authors of these papers on Nicolaitanism assumed that this is the same doctrine Christ spoke against.

Do you go to a church which governs from the top down; that is, the elders, deacons, priests, and so for, tell you what your contribution will be? Maybe you are in the wrong pew.

(18) And unto the angel of the church in Thyatira write, these things saith the Son of God, who hath his eyes like unto a flame of fire, and his feet are like fine brass.

(19) I know thy works, and charity, and service, and faith, and thy patience, and thy works; and the last to be more than the first.

(20) Notwithstanding I have a few things against thee, because thou suffered that woman Jezebel, which calleth herself a prophetess, to teach and to seduce my servants to commit fornication, and to eat things sacrificed unto idols.

(21) And I gave her space to repent of her fornication; and she repented not.

(22) Behold, I will cast her into a bed, and them that commit adultery with her into great tribulation, except they repent of their deeds.

(23) And I will kill her children with death; and all the churches shall know that I am he which searches the reins and hearts: and I will give unto every one of you according to your works.

(24) But unto you I say, and unto the rest in Thyatira, as many as have not this doctrine, and which have not known the depths of Satan, as they speak; I will put upon you none other burden.

(25) But that which ye have already hold fast till I come.

(26) And he that overcomes, and keeps my works unto the end, to him will I give power over the nations:

(27) And he shall rule them with a rod of iron; as the vessels of a potter shall they be broken to shivers: even as I received of my Father.

(28) And I will give him the morning star.

(29) He that hath an ear, let him hear what the Spirit saith unto the churches.

Chapter 10

Who is this Jezebel woman, Christ speaks against? I don't think it is a particular woman; just the actions of a type of person who thinks and behaves like the Jezebel of the Old Testament. If you can recall, she was the wife/ Queen of Ahab during his rein as King of Israel. The Spirit of Jezebel is what Christ is condemning and I will list a few of the things the Jezebel Spirit comprises.

Copied from:

10 CHARACTERISTICS OF THE JEZEBEL SPIRIT

AUGUST 5, 2019 | FROM CHARISMA NEWS

(1) The Jezebel spirit is always motivated by its own agenda, which it relentlessly pursues.

(2) The Jezebel spirit attacks, dominates, or manipulates, especially male authority. Queen Jezebel usurped political authority of the kingdom. This spirit's ultimate goal is to conquer or neutralize the prophet because a discerning leader is its greatest enemy.

(3) Jezebel causes fear, flight, and discouragement. This spirit often causes a spiritual leader to flee from his appointed place by character assassination and ruining his reputation.

(4) People under Jezebel's influence are natural leaders, although often covertly. The Jezebel spirit attempt to seek out people of influence to win their ear, gain credibility and win endorsement for their toxic cause.

(5) People under Jezebel's influence are often insecure and wounded, with pronounced egocentric needs. They are often trying to fill a love deficit. People under Jezebel's control always have deep, unhealed wounds from sources such as rejection, resistance, fear, insecurity, self-preservation, and

bitterness, which in turn, spreads its defilement to many.

(6) The Jezebel spirit functions subtlety and deceptively. People controlled by Jezebel use flattery to win you over to their domination. Jezebel spirits are masters of manipulation by guilt and undermining or discrediting another's influence. Those under Jezebel's control use flirtation and are extremely jealous of anyone they perceive to be a threat.

(7) Ultimately, people under Jezebel's influence are proud, independent, and rebellious. Rebellion is as the sin of witchcraft (1 Sam. 15:23) and will attempt to control others through any means other than the Holy Spirit.

(8) It takes an Ahab to let a Jezebel spirit operate unchallenged. Those under Jezebel's influence do not operate without someone under an Ahab spirit's influence enabling them to function.

(9) A Jezebel spirit is always in alignment with a religious spirit. Both Jezebel in the Old Testament and Revelation in the New Testament operated under the cover of religion. Its religious deeds are done for all to

see. True and pure spiritual gifts attract people to Jesus, not to the people who exercise the gifts.

(10) The families of people under Jezebel's influence are often out of order. Those under Jezebel's influence control their partners and cause their children to take sides, grow up insecure, disrespect their fathers, feel manipulated and become distrustful toward true authority.

Revelation Chapter three:

(1) And unto the angel of the church in Sardis write, these things saith he that hath the seven Spirits of God, and the seven stars; I know thy works, that thou hast a name that thou live, and art dead.

(2) Be watchful, and strengthen the things which remain, that are ready to die: for I have not found thy works perfect before God.

(3) Remember therefore how thou hast received and heard, and hold fast, and repent. If therefore thou shalt not watch, I will come on thee as a thief, and thou shalt not know what hour I will come upon thee.

(4) Thou hast a few names even in Sardis which have not defiled their garments; and they shall walk with me in white: for they are worthy.

(5) He that overcomes, the same shall be clothed in white raiment; and I will not blot out his name out of the book of life, but I will confess his name before my Father, and before his angels.

(6) He that hath an ear, let him hear what the Spirit saith unto the churches.

The church in Sardis is a good example of what we need to keep an eye out for in our modern churches today as well as in past history. It seems this church and a lot of churches today are guided by the fleshly wants ands desires. Their problem could be pursuing church growth and popularity instead of teaching God's truth and letting God give the growth for the church. This is just my opinion; the scripture doesn't give the exact faults of this church, let me remind you once again, the Catholic Church had sole control of the scriptures for 1260 years and could have removed parts that may have made them look bad. Again, just my thinking.

(7) And to the angel of the church in Philadelphia write, these things saith he that is holy, he that is true, he that hath the key of David, he that opens, and no man shuts; and shuts, and no man opens.

(8) I know thy works: behold, I have set before thee an open door, and no man can shut it: for thou hast a little strength, and hast kept my word, and hast not denied my name.

(9) Behold, I will make them of the synagogue of Satan, which say they are Jews, and are not, but do lie; behold, I will make them to come and worship before thy feet, and to know that I have loved thee.

(10) Because thou hast kept the word of my patience, I also will keep thee from the hour of temptation, which shall come upon all the world, to try them that dwell upon the earth.

(11) Behold, I come quickly: hold that fast which thou hast, that no man takes thy crown.

(12) Him that overcomes will I make a pillar in the temple of my God, and he shall go no more out: and I will write upon him the name of my God, and the name of the city of my God, which is new Jerusalem, which cometh down out of heaven from my God: and I will write upon him my new name.

(13) He that hath an ear, let him hear what the Spirit saith unto the churches.

Finally, a church God is proud of. They are doing things right. Christ finds no fault in this church. It seems like these church members have studied God's word and are doing the things he approves of. Just a quick question? Who are the ones who claim to be Jews but are not? The Kenites; Cain's descendants. Yes, they are still around.

(14) And unto the angel of the church of the Laodiceans write; These things saith the Amen, the faithful and true witness, the beginning of the creation of God.

(15) I know thy works, that thou art neither cold nor hot: I would thou wert cold or hot.

(16) So then because thou art lukewarm, and neither cold nor hot, I will spue thee out of my mouth.

(17) Because thou sayest, I am rich, and increased with goods, and have need of nothing; and knows not that thou art wretched, and miserable, and poor, and blind, and naked:

(18) I counsel thee to buy of me gold tried in the fire, that thou mayest be rich; and white raiment, that thou mayest be clothed, and that the shame of thy nakedness does not appear; and anoint thine eyes with eye salve, that thou mayest see.

(19) As many as I love, I rebuke and chasten, be zealous therefore, and repent.

(20) Behold, I stand at the door, and knock: if any man hears my voice, and open the door, I will come into him, and will sup with him, and he with me.

(21) To him that overcomes will I grant to sit with me in my throne, even as I also overcame, and am set down with my Father in his throne.

(22) He that hath an ear, let him hear what the Spirit saith unto the churches.

What can you do with people who just don't care one way or another? Oh, these types have plenty of money and property and they think this is enough; perhaps it is in this short flesh life, but where will they be when the flesh plays out?

After John has witness Christ preaching against the 7 churches, he sees a door open to Heaven and a voice inviting him to come to Heaven. Upon entering, he was immediately in the spirit and saw a throne with 4 beast and 24 elders clothed in white raiment surrounding the throne.

Revelation 4:5-7

(5) And out of the throne proceeded lightnings and thundering and voices: and there were seven lamps of fire burning before the throne, which are the seven Spirits of God.

(6) And before the throne there was a sea of glass like unto crystal: and in the midst of the throne, and round about the throne, were four beasts full of eyes before and behind.

(7) And the first beast was like a lion, and the second beast like a calf, and the third beast had a face as a man, and the fourth beast was like a flying eagle.

John sees a little book in the hand of the one sitting on the throne and no one is able to open the book except Christ.

Revelation 5:4-7

(4) And I wept much, because no man was found worthy to open and to read the book, neither to look thereon.

(5) And one of the elders saith unto me, Weep not: behold, the Lion of the tribe of Juda, the Root of David, hath prevailed to open the book, and to loose the seven seals thereof.

(6) And I beheld, and, lo, in the midst of the throne and of the four beasts, and in the midst of the elders, stood a Lamb as it had been slain, having seven horns and seven eyes, which are the seven Spirits of God sent forth into all the earth.

(7) And he came and took the book out of the right hand of him that sat upon the throne.

The rest of this chapter 5 is used in praises for Christ (Lamb) and for the sacrifice he made for his children. In the next chapter, that is, chapter 6, we see different types of horses portraying what is happening in the flesh world and what has happened and what will happen in the future of the flesh world.

Revelation chapter 6

(1) And I saw when the Lamb opened one of the seals, and I heard, as it were the noise of thunder, one of the four beasts saying, Come and see.

(2) And I saw and behold a white horse: and he that sat on him had a bow; and a crown was given unto him: and he went forth conquering, and to conquer.

(3) And when he had opened the second seal, I heard the second beast say, Come and see.

(4) And there went out another horse that was red: and power was given to him that sat thereon to take peace from the earth, and that they should kill one another: and there was given unto him a great sword.

(5) And when he had opened the third seal, I heard the third beast say, Come and see. And I beheld, and lo a black horse; and he that sat on him had a pair of balances in his hand.

(6) And I heard a voice in the midst of the four beasts say, A measure of wheat for a penny, and three measures of barley for a penny; and see thou hurt not the oil and the wine.

(7) And when he had opened the fourth seal, I heard the voice of the fourth beast say, Come and see.

(8) And I looked and behold a pale horse: and his name that sat on him was Death, and Hell followed with him. And power was given unto them over the fourth part of the earth, to kill with sword, and with hunger, and with death, and with the beasts of the earth.

The one riding the white horse is Satan. He's disguised as the Christ and is trying to influence people to listen to his ideas and to do things his way. Where is this happening? It's in your churches and governments and charity events, wherever people are trying to live for Christ. He's riding a white horse alright and has a bow surrounding him. The bow is not an archer's weapon, but the type of bow used on a present or package. Where our Lord was surrounded by all the different colors of a rainbow, (And he that sat was to look upon like a jasper and a sardine stone: and there was a rainbow round about the throne, in sight like unto an emerald.) Satan has around him a cheap fabric. Bow is translated from the Greek word, Toxon. It is where we get our English word, Toxic.

The next seal is Satan also; he just disguised as a war machine. Throughout our physical history, what has caused all the wars and human suffering? People trying to take something from another which didn't belong to them. It started with Cain killing Abel. Why? Abel had something Cain wanted. What did Abel have that caused Cain to murder him? Simply, the love of God and praise from our Father. Cain, like all dictators wanted to be put on a pedestal and worshipped because he thought he was better than anybody else.

The third horse is black in color. Black represents misery and famine, desperation. All these things are caused by the actions of the first two horses. So, we can say this black horse is also Satan in disguise. Wherever war and destruction occur, the black horse is close behind.

The fourth horse is a pale horse; Who is riding him? Death: we all know death is just another name for Satan. It says Hell followed him; since our notion of Hell doesn't exist, what is following this pale horse. Maybe, I should ask, what follows war and destruction? Most times, cities are destroyed, and the dead bodies pile up and disease is rampart, along with looting, raping, food shortage, complete anarchy. And God will allow this to take place if his children won't listen to his words of warnings. How about you, will you listen to your Fathers warnings?

Continuing in Revelation chapter 6:9-17

(9) And when he had opened the fifth seal, I saw under the altar the souls of them that were slain for the word of God, and for the testimony which they held:

(10) And they cried with a loud voice, saying, how long, O Lord, holy and true, dost thou not judge and avenge our blood on them that dwell on the earth?

(11) And white robes were given unto every one of them; and it was said unto them, that they should rest yet for a little season, until their fellow servants also and their brethren, that should be killed as they were, should be fulfilled.

(12) And I beheld when he had opened the sixth seal, and, lo, there was a great earthquake; and the sun became black as sackcloth of hair, and the moon became as blood.

John says when Christ opened the sixth seal, there was a great earthquake. We know or should know that when Satan sets up his Kingdom on earth; all things will change. The sun becoming 'black' simply means the inhabitants on earth will start to morn. The moon becoming as blood tells us a lot of blood will be shed under Satan's rule.

(13) And the stars of heaven fell unto the earth, even as a fig tree casts her untimely figs, when she is shaken of a mighty wind.

What or who are the stars? Simple put; they are the angels of God. In this case, bad angels who come to earth to help Satan achieve his goal. This is assured by the comment, of 'a fig tree casting out her untimely figs'. No angel is allowed to come to earth without a direct order from God; these came without permission.

(14) And the heaven departed as a scroll when it is rolled together; and every mountain and island were moved out of their places.

Heaven rolled together and departed means this is not the work of our Heavenly Father. Mountains are referring to earthly governments and the authority each Nation carries with its National borders. Islands are the little Nations and so forth. All world governments come under the authority of the Anti-Christ (Satan).

(15) And the kings of the earth, and the great men, and the rich men, and the chief captains, and

the mighty men, and every bondman, and every free man, hid themselves in the dens and in the rocks of the mountains.

Do you know who or what the 'kings of the earth' refer to? Think; what controls each or every worldly empire on earth? Give up? Here is the list; you can accept what I think or not. All kingdoms have these four things in order to rule. 1st is Government of some kind. Without some sort of government control, there would be anarchy. 2nd is financial, without a medium of exchange, there would be chaos. 3rd is education, all people in a controlled group have to be taught to obey the rules and what are the rules. Can you guess the fourth? It's probably not what you are thinking. The 4th is religion; all people believe in something. It could be a god of sorts or in themselves. It could be in a family unit like the head of a family who makes all the decisions, etc. Think about; you'll see I'm right.

(16) And said to the mountains and rocks, fall on us, and hide us from the face of him that sits on the throne, and from the wrath of the Lamb:

(17) For the great day of his wrath is come; and who shall be able to stand?

They are scared of the wrong lamb; this lamb is Satan, the antichrist. They are scared because Satan is pretending to be the Christ and because of his pretentious identity, they are afraid he'll take all the money and power away from them and so they want to hide, hoping he'll leave them alone. Always keep in mind, Satan comes at the sixth seal, six trump, six vials, as we'll see later on. In this time frame, it's only the six seal. I guess right now is a good time to explain the seal, trumps, and vials; a seal is portraying something that hasn't happened as yet but will in the future. The trump is the action taken when the seals time has come. The vials are the result of the actions of the seals and trumps. Got it!

Revelation chapter 7

Chapter seven is an insert chapter; God stops all things from happening until some of the things he wants done is taken care of. And what needs to be taken care of now?

(1) And after these things I saw four angels standing on the four corners of the earth, holding the four winds of the earth, that the wind should not blow on the earth, nor on the sea, nor on any tree.

(2) And I saw another angel ascending from the east, having the seal of the living God: and he cried with a loud voice to the four angels, to whom it was given to hurt the earth and the sea,

(3) Saying, hurt not the earth, neither the sea, nor the trees, till we have sealed the servants of our God in their foreheads.

The four angels holding back the four winds is symbolic of the end of this flesh age. God has a lot of believers living on earth in the flesh and he won't allow Satan to mess with them. So, to protect these, he seals their minds, so they won't be tempted into believing Satan's lies. The angel lists the number from the tribe of Israel and states there are thousands upon thousands who hold fast to God's word besides the one from the Nation of Israel.

Revelation chapter 8

(1) And when he had opened the seventh seal, there was silence in heaven about the space of half an hour.

You remember, I informed you Satan comes at the 6th seal; well, guess who comes at the 7th seal? Well, I'll tell you; it's Jesus the Christ, our savior and King. Now you know why there is silence in Heaven; Our King is going to return to save his people.

(2) And I saw the seven angels which stood before God; and to them were given seven trumpets.

(3) And another angel came and stood at the altar, having a golden censer; and there was given unto him much incense, that he should offer it with the prayers of all saints upon the golden altar which was before the throne.

Do you think God forgets your prayers? No; he doesn't.

(4) And the smoke of the incense, which came with the prayers of the saints, ascended up before God out of the angel's hand.

(5) And the angel took the censer, and filled it with fire of the altar, and cast it into the earth: and there were voices, and thundering, and lightnings, and an earthquake.

The start of Christ taking over the earth!

(6) And the seven angels which had the seven trumpets prepared themselves to sound.

(7) The first angel sounded, and there followed hail and fire mingled with blood, and they were cast upon the earth: and the third part of trees was burnt up, and all green grass was burnt up.

(8) And the second angel sounded, and as it were a great mountain burning with fire was cast into the sea: and the third part of the sea became blood.

(9) And the third part of the creatures which were in the sea, and had life, died; and the third part of the ships were destroyed.

(10) And the third angel sounded, and there fell a great star from heaven, burning as it were a lamp, and it fell upon the third part of the rivers, and upon the fountains of waters,

(11) And the name of the star is called Wormwood: and the third part of the waters became wormwood; and many men died of the waters, because they were made bitter.

(12) And the fourth angel sounded, and the third part of the sun was smitten, and the third part of the moon, and the third part of the stars; so, as the third part of them was darkened, and the day shone not for a third part of it, and the night likewise.

(13) And I beheld, and heard an angel flying through the midst of heaven, saying with a loud voice, Woe, woe, woe, to the inhibiters of the earth by reason of the other voices of the trumpet of the three angels, which are yet to sound!

Keep in focus; the seals are what God is planning. I see the trees and grass burning up to be a great natural disaster to take place on earth; famine and anarchy will reign and most of the world will be hungry and trying to find food anywhere they can locate it. Water is symbolic of people; so, I would think a sea would be a great multitude of people. A great mountain burning with fire probably means a large Nation will be overthrown and a third of its people will be killed. Same with verse 9, 10,11, 12, and 13; commerce will be destroyed. The star falling from heaven gives credence to the knowledge of God being behind all this chaos. Are you scared? You shouldn't be if you are one of God's faithful believers. Remember the Hebrew children in the book of Daniel who were thrown into a furnace of fire heated seven times hotter than necessary?

Daniel 3:21-25

(21) Then these men were bound in their coats, their hosen, and their hats, and their other garments, and were cast into the midst of the burning fiery furnace.

(22) Therefore, because the king's commandment was urgent, and the furnace exceeding

hot, the flame of the fire slew those men that took up Shadrach, Meshach, and Abednego.

(23) And these three men, Shadrach, Meshach, and Abednego, fell down bound into the midst of the burning fiery furnace.

(24) Then Nebuchadnezzar the king was astonied, and rose up in haste, and spoke, and said unto his counsellors, did not we cast three men bound into the midst of the fire? They answered and said unto the king, True, O king.

(25) He answered and said, Lo, I see four men loose, walking in the midst of the fire, and they have not been hurt; and the form of the fourth is like the Son of God.

The flames didn't hurt them because Christ protected them; He'll do the same for you if you are one of his children.

Zechariah 14:12

(12) And this shall be the plague wherewith the LORD will smite all the people that have fought against Jerusalem; Their flesh shall consume away

while they stand upon their feet, and their eyes shall consume away in their holes, and their tongue shall consume away in their mouth.

Chapter 11

(1) And the fifth angel sounded, and I saw a star fall from heaven unto the earth: and to him was given the key to the bottomless pit.

(2) And he opened the bottomless pit; and there arose a smoke out of the pit, as the smoke of a great furnace; and the sun and the air were darkened by reason of the smoke of the pit.

(3) And there came out of the smoke locusts upon the earth: and unto them was given power, as the scorpions of the earth have power.

(4) And it had commanded them that they should not hurt the grass of the earth, neither any green thing, neither any tree; but only those men which have not the seal of God in their foreheads

(5) And to them it was given that they should not kill them, but that they should be tormented five months: and their torment was as the torment of a scorpion, when he strikes a man.

(6) And in those days shall men seek death and shall not find it; and shall desire to die, and death shall flee from them.

(7) And the shapes of the locusts were like unto horses prepared unto battle; and on their heads were as it were crowns like gold, and their faces were as the faces of men.

(8) And they had hair as the hair of women, and their teeth were as the teeth of lions.

(9) And they had breastplates, as it were breastplates of iron; and the sound of their wings was as the sound of chariots of many horses running to battle.

(10) And they had tails like unto scorpions, and there were stings in their tails: and their power was to hurt men five months.

(11) And they had a king over them, which is the angel of the bottomless pit, whose name in the Hebrew tongue is Abaddon, but in the Greek tongue hath his name Apollyon.

A star falling from heaven would seem to me to be a fallen angel; one of Satan's bunch. Don't lose focus; this is what our God is planning for the future. This angel was given the key to the bottomless pit and when it was opened, what came out.? A great smoke as of a great furnace. The smoke was so great that it dimmed then sun and air.

When I was a young lad and listening to sales pitches from different people, my brother reminded me to "not let them blow smoke up my butt"; meaning, a con game was afoot.

So, this smoke is a con game put out by Satan and all the other objects coming out of the 'pit' are also devices used by Satan in his attempt to hold power on the earth and to defeat our Christ.

The so-called Locust are ordered to leave everything along except the people who don't have the seal of God in their forehead. What is in your forehead? Your brain or maybe I should say your mind. The place where you do your thinking.

How long will the Lord allow this action of Satan to continue? The bible says five months. The bible also said men will seek to die but death will flee from them. Why? When our Christ returns and his feet touches the ground, all flesh will be dissolved, and everybody will be changed into a spiritual body. Only God can kill a spiritual body.

We are told, this demonic bunch has a king over them, and his name is Abaddon in the Hebrew and his name in the Greek is Apollyon. The name translated to English is 'destroyer' from the Greek and the same thing from the Hebrew, a 'destroyer'; meaning Satan, whereas destroyer is one of his names.

(12) One woe is past; and behold, there come two woes more hereafter.

(13) And the sixth angel sounded, and I heard a voice from the four horns of the golden altar, which is before God,

The four horns are symbols of power. Being of the golden altar lets us know, the power belongs to God. And the voice telling the sixth angel to loose the four angels bound in the river Euphrates means the world is about to experience world-wide chaos. The River, Euphrates has always been a dividing line between God's people and the Atheist world or Satan's dominion.

(14) Saying to the sixth angel which had the trumpet, Loose the four angels which are bound in the great river Euphrates.

(15) And the four angels were loosed, which were prepared for an hour, and a day, and a month, and a year, for to slay the third part of men.

(16) And the number of the army of the horsemen were two hundred thousand thousand: and I heard the number of them.

(17) And thus, I saw the horses in the vision, and them that sat on them, having breastplates of fire, and of jacinth, and brimstone: and the heads of the horses were as the heads of lions; and out of their mouths issued fire and smoke and brimstone.

The horsemen are symbolic of different Nations' war-machines and troops being called into war with Satan controlling them. Have you ever seen a city after a bombing raid? It's on fire and is burning up; smoke is a propaganda machine which all nations use in war time; it's to make the enemy lose the desire to fight. Jacinth represents the money needed to pay the troops and to buy more ammo. Of course, the brimstone is symbolic of bombs being dropped on the people.

(18) By these three was the third part of men killed, by the fire, and by the smoke, and by the brimstone, which issued out of their mouths.

(19) For their power is in their mouth, and in their tails: for their tails were like unto serpents, and had heads, and with them they do hurt.

(20) And the rest of the men which were not killed by these plagues yet repented not of the works of their hands, that they should not worship devils, and idols of gold, and silver, and brass, and stone, and of wood: which neither can see, nor hear, nor walk:

(21) Neither repented they of their murders, nor of their sorceries, nor of their fornication, nor of their thefts.

Revelation, chapter ten:

(1) And I saw another mighty angel come down from heaven, clothed with a cloud: and a rainbow was upon his head, and his face was as it were the sun, and his feet as pillars of fire:

This is a different type of angel than the last one. This is a messenger from God; we know because of the description. The angel doesn't fall' from

Heaven, it has a rainbow around it's head and has a bright face like the sun and his feet as pillars of fire. Would you not say this is the Christ?

"And his feet like unto fine brass, as if they burned in a furnace; and his voice as the sound of many waters." (Rev. 1:14)

(2) And he had in his hand a little book open: and he set his right foot upon the sea, and his left foot on the earth,

(3) And cried with a loud voice, as when a lion roared: and when he had cried, seven thunders uttered their voices.

(4) And when the seven thunders had uttered their voices, I was about to write: and I heard a voice from heaven saying unto me, seal up those things which the seven thunders uttered, and write them not.

Why would the angel not allow John to write what the seven thunders said? It's already in the bible. Read Psalm 29 and I think you'll agree with me about the thunders.

Psalm 29:3-9

(3) The voice of the LORD is upon the waters: The God of glory thundered: the LORD is upon many waters.

(4) The voice of the LORD is powerful; the voice of the LORD is full of majesty.

(5) The voice of the LORD breaks the cedars; yea, the LORD breaks the cedars of Lebanon.

(6) He makes them also to skip like a calf; Lebanon and Sirion like a young unicorn.

(7) The voice of the LORD divides the flames of fire.

(8) The voice of the LORD shakes the wilderness; the LORD shakes the wilderness of Kadesh.

(9) The voice of the LORD makes the hinds to calve and discovered the forests: and in his temple doth everyone speaks of his glory.

The voice of the Lord is the thunder and as it says in Psalm 29, it is the seven thunders.

Now back to Rev. chapter ten:

(5) And the angel which I saw stand upon the sea and upon the earth lifted up his hand to heaven,

(6) And swear by him that lives for ever and ever, who created heaven, and the things that therein are, and the earth, and the things that therein are, and the sea, and the things which are therein, that there should be time no longer:

(7) But in the days of the voice of the seventh angel, when he shall begin to sound, the mystery of God should be finished, as he hath declared to his servants the prophets.

As we say down South, the 'fat lady sings', meaning it's all over but the shouting for joy because our King has returned and taken control of everything in Heaven and Earth.

(8) And the voice which I heard from heaven spoke unto me again, and said, Go and take the little book which is open in the hand of the angel which stands upon the sea and upon the earth.

(9) And I went unto the angel, and said unto him, Give me the little book. And he said unto me, take it, and eat it up; and it shall make thy belly bitter, but it shall be in thy mouth sweet as honey.

(10) And I took the little book out of the angel's hand and ate it up; and it was in my mouth sweet as honey: and as soon as I had eaten it, my belly was bitter.

(11) And he said unto me, thou must prophesy again before many peoples, and nations, and tongues, and kings.

What is the little book? It shows have God plans to make the end of this earth age come to a final stop. At first, John is glad to know how the end will come about but is then sad because of all the ones who don't make it into life eternal. Where will you be? The choice is ours. This ends our look at the seals, the way God plans to let happen, but it hasn't happened yet, at least not everything given here. Now we'll look at the trumps and get an idea from our knowledge of history as to where we are in God's timeline.

Revelation chapter 11

I call this eleventh chapter an insert chapter. Our Heavenly Father wants us to learn a few things or to remember some things before he goes on with the seventh trump. The Temple of God, where is it? John, the apostle, is in the spirit and in Heaven; he's there to write what he sees and as a witness to what our Heavenly Father is planning for the future of his children. He has basically let them alone in the flesh body for almost seven thousand years as we measure time. God measures time different than we in the flesh measure time as you'll see.

(1) And there was given me a reed like unto a rod: and the angel stood, saying, Rise, and measure the temple of God, and the altar, and them that worship therein.

The angel escorting John around Heaven gives John a reed, like a rod, in our understanding, a measuring device. The angel instructs John to measure the Temple of God the altar, and the ones who worship in the Temple.

(2) But the court, which is without the temple leave out, and measure it not; for it is given unto the Gentiles: and the holy city shall they tread under foot forty and two months.

Where is the 'holy city'? It is in Heaven, also. We know because John is still in Heaven. Do you still have it fixed in your mind where Christ went at his death on the cross?

Peter 4:6

(6) For this cause was the gospel preached also to them that are dead, that they might be judged according to men in the flesh but live according to God in the spirit.

Matthew 27:52-53

(52) And the graves were opened; and many bodies of the saints which slept arose,

(53) And came out of the graves after his resurrection, and went into the holy city, and appeared unto many.

Why are these dead souls? They are dead because of the sin of Adam when he disobeyed God in the 'Garden of Eden'; since that day, all souls have been held across the vast gulf waiting for someone to pay their sin debt and they could be released. God did this himself in the human form of Jesus the Christ.

When Christ preached to these spirits or souls, many believed on him and were released from the dead place, (across the vast gulf) and they walked the streets of the Holy City. It is interesting to note, there were a lot of Gentiles in the dead place who believed on Christ and they were allowed into the Holy City and 'appeared to many' for 42 months, which equals 1260 days or 1260 years; the exact same time the Catholic Church had control of the scriptures and all religious services. That is, from 538 AD until 1798 AD.

Revelation 11:3

(3) And I will give power unto my two witnesses, and they shall prophesy a thousand two hundred and threescore days, clothed in sackcloth.

Note: 1260 days equal the same 1260 years as the 42 months; 538 to 1798. I look on these two witnesses as being the true word of God. Clothed in sackcloth represents the beggarly role of the true worship of God.

Have you not figured out the two witness yet? Well, I'll tell you; they are the Old Testament, or perhaps I should say Moses and Elijah or the 'Law' and the 'Prophets'.

I came to this conclusion by remembering who were on the 'Mount of Transfiguration' with Jesus. The bible lets us know it was Moses and Elijah. Elijah never died in the physical body and I don't think Moses did either. Why? In the book of Jude, Satan contends with the Arch Angel, Michael about the body of Moses; Satan wanted to know where God buried Moses. Satan knew Moses deserved the physical death because he was a sinner, but Michael wouldn't even discuss the matter, he just told Satan to take it up with God.

Jude 1:9

(9) Yet Michael the archangel, when contending with the devil he disputed about the body of Moses, durst not bring against him a railing accusation, but said, The Lord rebuke thee.

Revelation 11:4

(4) These are the two olive trees, and the two candlesticks standing before the God of the earth.

Olives Trees are Moses and Elijah, and the two candlesticks are the two churches which Christ was pleased by what they taught; that is the true message of Christ. See Rev. 2:9 and 3:9

Revelation 11:5

(5) And if any man will hurt them, fire proceeded out of their mouth, and devoured their

enemies: and if any man will hurt them, he must in this manner be killed.

(6) These have power to shut heaven, that it rains not in the days of their prophecy: and have power over waters to turn them to blood, and to smite the earth with all plagues, as often as they will.

(7) And when they shall have finished their testimony, the beast that ascended out of the bottomless pit shall make war against them, and shall overcome them, and kill them.

(8) And their dead bodies shall lie in the street of the great city, which spiritually is called Sodom and Egypt, where also our Lord was crucified.

The scripture doesn't say these two witnesses will do the things listed above; it just lets us know they have the power to do these things. In my opinion, these two witnesses arrive on the scene after Satan has taken over the Earth as ruler with all the world believing him to be the Christ.

Revelation 13:8

(8) And all that dwell upon the earth shall worship him, whose names are not written in the book of life of the Lamb slain from the foundation of the world.

Continuing with Revelation 11:9-19

(9) And they of the people and kindreds and tongues and nations shall see their dead bodies three days and a half and shall not suffer their dead bodies to be put in graves.

(10) And they that dwell upon the earth shall rejoice over them, and make merry, and shall send gifts one to another; because these two prophets tormented them that dwelt on the earth.

(11) And after three days and a half the Spirit of life from God entered into them, and they stood upon their feet; and great fear fell upon them which saw them.

(12) And they heard a great voice from heaven saying unto them, Come up hither. And they ascended up to heaven in a cloud; and their enemies beheld them.

(13) And the same hour was there a great earthquake, and the tenth part of the city fell, and in the earthquake were slain of men seven thousand: and the remnant were affrighted and gave glory to the God of heaven.

(14) The second woe is past; and behold, the third woe cometh quickly.

The peoples of the world believe Satan is Christ and the things he does is good for all mankind. So, when Satan has these two witnesses killed, they believe he has gotten rid of all opposition to them having a great life. But after three and a half days, their joy turns to great fear; the two witnesses come back to life and ascend up to Heaven.

(15) And the seventh angel sounded; and there were great voices in heaven, saying, the kingdoms of this world are become the kingdoms of our Lord, and of his Christ; and he shall reign for ever and ever.

(16) And the four and twenty elders, which sat before God on their seats, fell upon their faces, and worshipped God,

(17) Saying, we give thee thanks, O Lord God Almighty, which art, and was, and art to come; because thou hast taken to thee thy great power, and hast reigned.

(18) And the nations were angry, and thy wrath is come, and the time of the dead, that they should be judged, and that thou shouldest give reward unto thy servants the prophets, and to the saints, and them that fear thy name, small and great; and shouldest destroy them which destroy the earth.

(19) And the temple of God was opened in heaven, and there was seen in his temple the ark of his testament: and there were lightnings, and voices, and thundering's, and an earthquake, and great hail.

The fat lady has sung and it's all over but the removing of Satan from his role as King of earth.

Chapter 12

This chapter starts at the beginning of time as it states if the first chapter of the book of John.

(1) And there appeared a great wonder in heaven; a woman clothed with the sun, and the moon under her feet, and upon her head a crown of twelve stars:

This is God's plan to bring in a whole new creation. The woman (new creation) giving birth to this creation by the sun (God) with the moon (Angel of God) in full accord.

(2) And she, being with child cried, travailing in birth, and pained to be delivered.

(3) And there appeared another wonder in heaven; and behold a great red dragon, having seven heads and ten horns, and seven crowns upon his heads.

We'll learn in the next few verses this Red Dragon is symbolic of Satan; that is, this is just one of his many titles. The seven heads represent the seven different kingdoms he will set up on earth to draw God's children away from our Heavenly Father. Horns always portray power, usually a monarch of some country or kingdom. The crowns are the kings of these countries.

(4) And his tail drew the third part of the stars of heaven and did cast them to the earth: and the dragon stood before the woman, which was ready to be delivered, for to devour her child as soon as it was born.

We have already been informed; the stars are angels. So, this means Satan seduced a third of God's angels to follow him in a rebellion against God. In this verse, the woman has become Mary, the mother of Jesus and Satan tried to kill the Christ child as soon as it was born. He did this through Herod, King of Judaea, when Herod gave the order for all the children born in Bethlehem to be killed, hoping one of them would be Jesus.

(5) And she brought forth a man child, who was to rule all nations with a rod of iron: and her child was caught up unto God, and to his throne.

(6) And the woman fled into the wilderness, where she hath a place prepared of God, that they should feed her there a thousand two hundred and threescore days.

The wilderness turns out to be the Catholic Church at this time and the woman is Christianity. This is the same 1260 years the Roman government gave absolute authority to the Papacy in all matters concerning the law of the Roman Empire, from 538 AD until 1798 AD.

(7) And there was war in heaven: Michael and his angels fought against the dragon; and the dragon fought and his angels,

This verse 7 is out of place; it should follow verse 4 because this took place before the first verse of Genesis. The war in Heaven is the reason for the creation of this physical age in the first place.

(8) And prevailed not; neither was their place found any more in heaven.

(9) And the great dragon was cast out, that old serpent, called the Devil, and Satan, which deceives the whole world: he was cast out into the earth, and his angels were cast out with him.

(10) And I heard a loud voice saying in heaven, Now is come salvation, and strength, and the kingdom of our God, and the power of his Christ: for the accuser of our brethren is cast down, which accused them before our God day and night.

(11) And they overcame him by the blood of the Lamb, and by the word of their testimony; and they loved not their lives unto the death.

(12) Therefore rejoice, ye heavens, and ye that dwell in them. Woe to the inhibiters of the earth and of the sea! for the devil is come down unto you, having great wrath, because he knows that he hath but a short time.

(13) And when the dragon saw that he was cast unto the earth, he persecuted the woman which brought forth the man child.

(14) And to the woman were given two wings of a great eagle, that she might fly into the wilderness, into her place, where she is nourished for a time, and times, and half a time, from the face of the serpent.

A time equals one year in God's calendar, that makes a time plus times (two years) and a half a time (1/2 year) becomes 3 and ½ years; or 42 months or 1260 days which equal 1260 years or the same as we had before. The years from 538 AD until 1798 AD.

(15) And the serpent cast out of his mouth water as a flood after the woman, that he might cause her to be carried away of the flood.

(16) And the earth helped the woman, and the earth opened her mouth, and swallowed up the flood which the dragon cast out of his mouth.

(17) And the dragon was wroth with the woman and went to make war with the remnant of her seed, which keep the commandments of God, and have the testimony of Jesus Christ.

The Catholic Church tried to keep knowledge of the bible and what it proclaims solely within the knowledge of the Papacy and the Priests, but the people wanted their own bibles to read and study. Under King James of England, the bible was translated to an English version for all his subjects to read and have a copy.

Rev. chapter 13

(1) And I stood upon the sand of the sea, and saw a beast rise up out of the sea, having seven heads and ten horns, and upon his horns ten crowns, and upon his heads the name of blasphemy.

This is a copy or image of the 'Dragon' we were introduced to in the last chapter. Only here it is a physical organization, where before it was a super-natural beast; that is, Satan. It is made up on the historical kingdoms which ruled humanity in the past. It has the speed of a leopard, (Alexander the Great) feet of a bear, (Medo-Persian) mouth of a lion, (Nebuchadnezzar). But always keep in mind, Satan controls this Beast.

(2) And the beast which I saw was like unto a leopard, and his feet were as the feet of a bear, and his mouth as the mouth of a lion: and the dragon gave him his power, and his seat, and great authority.

(3) And I saw one of his heads as it were wounded to death; and his deadly wound was healed: and all the world wondered after the beast.

This is the same Beast we learned about in the book of Daniel and in the 12th chapter of Revelation, just a little bit different description this time.

(4) And they worshipped the dragon which gave power unto the beast: and they worshipped the beast, saying, who is like unto the beast? who is able to make war with him?

(5) And there was given unto him a mouth speaking great things and blasphemies; and power was given unto him to continue forty and two months.

(6) And he opened his mouth in blasphemy against God, to blaspheme his name, and his tabernacle, and them that dwell in heaven.

42 months equal 1260 days equal 1260 years. This is the same beast we have already studied.

(7) And it was given unto him to make war with the saints, and to overcome them: and power was given him over all kindreds, and tongues, and nations.

(8) And all that dwell upon the earth shall worship him, whose names are not written in the book of life of the Lamb slain from the foundation of the world.

(9) If any man has an ear, let him hear.

(10) He that leadeth into captivity shall go into captivity: he that killed with the sword must be killed with the sword. Here is the patience and the faith of the saints.

(11) And I beheld another beast coming up out of the earth; and he had two horns like a lamb, and he spoke as a dragon.

A wild beast rises out of the sea, to whom the dragon gives his power. (1-10) Another beast, which has two horns like a lamb, but speaks as a dragon.

(11-15) It obliges all to worship its image, and receive its mark, as persons devoted to it. (16-18)1-10 The apostle, standing on the shore, saw a savage beast rise out of the sea; a tyrannical, idolatrous, persecuting power, springing up out of the troubles which took place. It was a frightful monster! It appears to mean that worldly, oppressing dominion, which for many ages, even from the times of the Babylonish captivity, had been hostile to the church. The first beast then began to oppress and persecute the righteous for righteousness' sake, but they suffered most under the fourth beast of Daniel, (the Roman empire,) which has afflicted the saints with many cruel persecutions. The source of its power was the dragon. It was set up by the devil and supported by him. The wounding the head may be the abolishing pagan idolatry; and the healing of the wound, introducing popish idolatry, the same in substance, only in a new dress, but which as effectually answers the devil's design. The world admired its power, policy, and success. They paid honor and subjection to the devil and his instruments. It exercised infernal power and policy, requiring men to render that honor to creatures which belongs to God alone. Yet the devil's power and success are limited. Christ has a chosen remnant, redeemed by his blood, recorded in his book, sealed by his Spirit; and though the devil and antichrist may overcome the body, and take away the natural life, they cannot conquer the soul, nor prevail with true believers to forsake their Savior, and join his enemies. Perseverance in the faith of the gospel and true worship of God, in this great hour of trial and temptation, which would deceive all but the elect, is the character of those registered in the book of life. This powerful motive and encouragement to constancy, is the great design of the whole Revelation.

Commentary by Matthew Henry 1710

(12) And he exercises all the power of the first beast before him and causes the earth and them which dwell therein to worship the first beast, whose deadly wound was healed.

(13) And he doeth great wonders, so that he makes fire come down from heaven on the earth in the sight of men,

(14) And deceives them that dwell on the earth by the means of those miracles which he had power to do in the sight of the beast; saying to them that dwell on the earth, that they should make an image to the beast, which had the wound by a sword, and did live.

(15) And he had power to give life unto the image of the beast, that the image of the beast should both speak, and cause that as many as would not worship the image of the beast should be killed.

(16) And he causes all, both small and great, rich, and poor, free and bond, to receive a mark in their right hand, or in their foreheads:

(17) And that no man might buy or sell, save he that had the mark, or the name of the beast, or the number of his name.

(18) Here is wisdom. Let him that hath understanding count the number of the beast: for it is

the number of a man; and his number is Six hundred threescore and six.

11-18 Those who understand the first beast to denote a worldly power, take the second to be also a persecuting and assumed power, which acts under the disguise of religion, and of charity to the souls of men. It is a spiritual dominion, professing to be derived from Christ, and exercised at first in a gentle manner, but soon spoke like the dragon. Its speech betrayed it; for it gives forth those false doctrines and cruel decrees, which show it to belong to the dragon, and not to the Lamb. It exercised all the power of the former beast. It pursues the same design, to draw men from worshipping the true God, and to subject the souls of men to the will and control of men. The second beast has carried on its designs, by methods whereby men should be deceived to worship the former beast, in the new shape, or likeness made for it. By lying wonders, pretended miracles. And by severe censures. Also, by allowing none to enjoy natural or civil rights, who will not worship that beast which is the image of the pagan beast. It is made a qualification for buying and selling, as well as for places of profit and trust, that they oblige themselves to use all their interest, power, and endeavor, to forward the dominion of the beast, which is meant by receiving his mark. To make an image to the beast, whose deadly wound was healed, would be to give form and power to his worship, or to require obedience to his commands. To worship the image of the beast, implies being subject to those things which stamp the character of the picture, and render it the image of the beast. The number of the beast is given, so as to show the infinite wisdom of God, and to exercise the wisdom of men. The number is the number of a man, computed after the usual manner among men, and it is 666. What or who is intended by this, remains a mystery. To almost every religious dispute this number has yet been applied, and it may reasonably be doubted whether the meaning has yet been discovered. But he who has wisdom and understanding, will see that all the enemies of God are numbered and marked out for destruction; that the term of their power will soon expire, and that all nations shall submit to our King of righteousness and peace.

Commentary by Matthew Henry, 1710.

These are the thoughts of Matthew Henry in the year 1710 AD. At that time, the Papacy was still in power and the time God allowed him to retain the power over the Roman Empire was not over as yet. It would survive until 1798 AD as stated before. As you read through Mr. Henry's commentary, I think you will agree with me his thoughts are very similar to mine; he just hadn't realized the bible was talking about the length of time allowed to the Papacy.

Revelation chapter 14

(1) And I looked, and, lo, a Lamb stood on the mount Zion, and with him a hundred forty and four thousand, having his Father's name written in their foreheads.

(2) And I heard a voice from heaven, as the voice of many waters, and as the voice of a great thunder: and I heard the voice of harpers harping with their harps:

(3) And they sung as it were a new song before the throne, and before the four beasts, and the elders: and no man could learn that song but the hundred and forty and four thousand, which were redeemed from the earth.

(4) These are they which were not defiled with women; for they are virgins. These are they which follow the Lamb whithersoever he goes. These were redeemed from among men, being the first fruits unto God and to the Lamb.

(5) And in their mouth was found no guile: for they are without fault before the throne of God.

(6) And I saw another angel fly in the midst of heaven, having the everlasting gospel to preach unto them that dwell on the earth, and to every nation, and kindred, and tongue, and people,

(7) Saying with a loud voice, Fear God, and give glory to him; for the hour of his judgment is come and

worship him that made heaven, and earth, and the sea, and the fountains of waters.

(8) And there followed another angel, saying, Babylon is fallen, is fallen, that great city, because she made all nations drink of the wine of the wrath of her fornication.

(9) And the third angel followed them, saying with a loud voice, if any man worships the beast and his image, and receive his mark in his forehead, or in his hand,

(10) The same shall drink of the wine of the wrath of God, which is poured out without mixture into the cup of his indignation; and he shall be tormented with fire and brimstone in the presence of the holy angels, and in the presence of the Lamb:

(11) And the smoke of their torment ascended up for ever and ever: and they have no rest day nor night, who worship the beast and his image, and whosoever receives the mark of his name.

(12) Here is the patience of the saints: here are they that keep the commandments of God, and the faith of Jesus.

(13) And I heard a voice from heaven saying unto me, Write, blessed are the dead which die in the Lord from henceforth: Yea, saith the Spirit, that they may rest from their labors; and their works do follow them.

(14) And I looked, and behold a white cloud, and upon the cloud one sat like unto the Son of man, having on his head a golden crown, and in his hand a sharp sickle.

(15) And another angel came out of the temple, crying with a loud voice to him that sat on the cloud, thrust in thy sickle, and reap, for the time is come for thee to reap; for the harvest of the earth is ripe.

(16) And he that sat on the cloud thrust in his sickle on the earth; and the earth was reaped.

(17) And another angel came out of the temple, which is in heaven, he also having a sharp sickle.

(18) And another angel came out from the altar, which had power over fire; and cried with a loud cry to him that had the sharp sickle, saying, thrust in thy sharp sickle, and gather the clusters of the vine of the earth; for her grapes are fully ripe.

(19) And the angel thrust in his sickle into the earth, and gathered the vine of the earth, and cast it into the great winepress of the wrath of God.

(20) And the winepress was trodden without the city, and blood came out of the winepress, even unto the horse bridles, by the space of a thousand and six hundred furlongs.

Those faithful to Christ celebrate the praises of God. (1-5) Three angels; one proclaiming the everlasting gospel; another, the downfall of Babylon; and a third, the dreadful wrath of God on the worshippers of the beast. The blessedness of those who die in the Lord. (6-13) A vision of Christ with a sickle, and of a harvest ripe for cutting down. (14-16) The emblem of a vintage fully ripe, trodden in the winepress of God's wrath. (17-20)1-5 Mount Sion is the gospel church. Christ is with his church, and in the midst of her in all her troubles, therefore she is not consumed. His presence secures perseverance. His people appear honorably. They have the name of God written in their foreheads; they make a bold and open profession of their faith in God and Christ, and this is followed by suitable actions. There were persons in the darkest times, who ventured and laid down their lives for the worship and truth of the gospel of Christ. They kept themselves clean from the wicked abominations of the followers of antichrist. Their hearts were right with God; and they were freely pardoned in Christ; he is glorified in them, and they in him. May it be our prayer, our endeavor, our ambition, to be found in this honorable company. Those who are really sanctified and justified are meant here, for no hypocrite, however plausible, can be accounted to be without fault before God.

6-13 The progress of the Reformation appears to be here set forth. The four proclamations are plain in their meaning; that all Christians may be encouraged, in the time of trial, to be faithful to their Lord. The gospel is the great means whereby men are brought to fear God, and to give glory to him. The preaching of the everlasting gospel shakes the foundations of antichrist in the world and hastens its downfall. If any persist in being subject to the beast, and in promoting his cause, they must expect to be forever miserable in soul and body. The believer is to venture or suffer any thing in obeying the commandments of God and professing the faith of Jesus. May God bestow this patience upon us. Observe the description of those that are and shall be blessed: such as die in the Lord; die in the cause of Christ, in a state of union with Christ, such as are found in Christ when death comes. They rest from all sin, temptation, sorrow, and persecution; for there, the wicked cease from troubling, there the weary are at rest. Their works follow them: do not go before as their title, or purchase, but follow them as proofs of their having lived and died in the Lord: the remembrance of them will be pleasant, and the reward far above all their services and sufferings. This is made sure by the testimony of the Spirit, witnessing with their spirits, and the written word.

14-20 Warnings and judgments not having produced reformation, the sins of the nations are filled up, and they become ripe for judgments, represented by a harvest, an emblem which is used to signify the gathering of the righteous, when ripe for heaven, by the mercy of God. The harvest time is when the corn is ripe; when the believers are ripe for heaven, then the wheat of the earth shall be gathered into Christ's garner. And by a vintage. The enemies of Christ and his church are not destroyed, till by their sin they are ripe for ruin, and then he will spare them no longer. The winepress is the wrath of God, some terrible calamity, probably the sword, shedding the blood of the wicked. The patience of God towards sinners, is the greatest miracle in the world; but, though lasting, it will not be everlasting; and ripeness in sin is a sure proof of judgment at hand.

Commentary by Matthew Henry, 1710.

Chapter 13

Revelation 15:1-4

(1) And I saw another sign in heaven, great and marvelous, seven angels having the seven last plagues; for in them is filled up the wrath of God.

(2) And I saw as it were a sea of glass mingled with fire: and them that had gotten the victory over the beast, and over his image, and over his mark, and over the number of his name, stand on the sea of glass, having the harps of God.

(3) And they sing the song of Moses the servant of God, and the song of the Lamb, saying, Great and

marvelous are thy works, Lord God Almighty; just and true are thy ways, thou King of saints.

(4) Who shall not fear thee, O Lord, and glorify thy name? for thou only art holy: for all nations shall come and worship before thee; for thy judgments are made manifest.

Keep in mind, sea, represents people; for the saved ones to look like a throng so great it would seem to mingle into one body or a 'sea of glass'.

Do you know the song they were singing; that is, the song of Moses? No! Well, you can find it in the Old Testament; it's in the book of Deuteronomy, chapter 32. But the title of the song is given in the last verse of Chapter 31:30.

(30) And Moses spoke in the ears of all the congregation of Israel the words of this song, until they were ended.

Now the song, Deuteronomy, chapter 32, verse one.

(1) Give ear, O ye heavens, and I will speak; and hear, O earth, the words of my mouth.

(2) My doctrine shall drop as the rain, my speech shall distil as the dew, as the small rain upon the tender herb, and as the showers upon the grass:

(3) Because I will publish the name of the LORD: ascribe ye greatness unto our God.

(4) He is the Rock, his work is perfect: for all his ways are judgment: A God of truth and without iniquity, just and right is he.

(5) They have corrupted themselves; their spot is not the spot of his children: they are a perverse and crooked generation.

(They) Are the ones who are non-believers. Satan followers.

(6) Do ye thus requite the LORD, O foolish people and unwise? is not he thy father that hath bought thee? hath he not made thee, and established thee?

(7) Remember the days of old, consider the years of many generations: ask thy father, and he will shew thee; thy elders, and they will tell thee.

(8) When the most High divided to the nations their inheritance, when he separated the sons of

Adam, he set the bounds of the people according to the number of the children of Israel.

(9) For the LORD'S portion is his people; Jacob is the lot of his inheritance.

(10) He found him in a desert land, and in the waste howling wilderness; he led him about, he instructed him, he kept him as the apple of his eye.

(11) As an eagle stirred up her nest, fluttered over her young, spreadiest abroad her wings, taketh them, bears them on her wings:

(12) So, the LORD alone did lead him, and there was no strange god with him.

(13) He made him ride on the high places of the earth, that he might eat the increase of the fields; and he made him to suck honey out of the rock, and oil out of the flinty rock.

(14) Butter of kine, and milk of sheep, with fat of lambs, and rams of the breed of Bashan, and goats, with the fat of kidneys of wheat; and thou didst drink the pure blood of the grape.

(15) But Jeshurun waxed fat, and kicked: thou art waxen fat, thou art grown thick, thou art covered

with fatness; then he forsook God which made him, and lightly esteemed the Rock of his salvation.

(16) They provoked him to jealousy with strange gods, with abominations provoked they him to anger.

(17) They sacrificed unto devils, not to God; to gods whom they knew not, to new gods that came newly up, whom your fathers feared not.

(18) Of the Rock that begat thee thou art unmindful, and hast forgotten God that formed thee.

(19) And when the LORD saw it, he abhorred them, because of the provoking of his sons, and of his daughters.

(20) And he said, I will hide my face from them, I will see what their end shall be: for they are a very froward generation, children in whom is no faith.

(21) They have moved me to jealousy with that which is not God; they have provoked me to anger with their vanities: and I will move them to jealousy with those which are not a people; I will provoke them to anger with a foolish nation.

(22) For a fire is kindled in mine anger, and shall burn unto the lowest hell, and shall consume the earth with her increase, and set on fire the foundations of the mountains.

(23) I will heap mischiefs upon them; I will spend mine arrows upon them.

(24) They shall be burnt with hunger, and devoured with burning heat, and with bitter destruction: I will also send the teeth of beasts upon them, with the poison of serpents of the dust.

(25) The sword without, and terror within, shall destroy both the young man and the virgin, the suckling also with the man of gray hairs.

(26) I said, I would scatter them into corners, I would make the remembrance of them to cease from among men:

(27) Were it not that I feared the wrath of the enemy, lest their adversaries should behave themselves strangely, and lest they should say, our hand is high, and the LORD hath not done all this.

(28) For they are a nation void of counsel, neither is there any understanding in them.

(29) O that they were wise, that they understood this, that they would consider their latter end!

(30) How should one chase a thousand, and two put ten thousand to flight, except their Rock had sold them, and the LORD had shut them up?

(31) For their rock is not as our Rock, even our enemies themselves being judges.

(32) For their vine is of the vine of Sodom, and of the fields of Gomorrah: their grapes are grapes of gall, their clusters are bitter:

(33) Their wine is the poison of dragons, and the cruel venom of asps.

(34) Is not this laid up in store with me, and sealed up among my treasures?

(35) To me belongs vengeance, and recompence; their foot shall slide in due time: for the day of their calamity is at hand, and the things that shall come upon them make haste.

(36) For the LORD shall judge his people, and repent himself for his servants, when he sees that their power is gone, and there is none shut up, or left.

(37) And he shall say, where are their gods, their rock in whom they trusted,

(38) Which did eat the fat of their sacrifices and drank the wine of their drink offerings? let them rise up and help you and be your protection.

(39) See now that I, even I, am he, and there is no god with me: I kill, and I make alive; I wound, and I heal: neither is there any that can deliver out of my hand.

(40) For I lift up my hand to heaven, and say, I live forever.

(41) If I whet my glittering sword, and mine hand take hold on judgment; I will render vengeance to mine enemies and will reward them that hate me.

(42) I will make mine arrows drunk with blood, and my sword shall devour flesh; and that with the blood of the slain and of the captives, from the beginning of revenges upon the enemy.

(43) Rejoice, O ye nations, with his people: for he will avenge the blood of his servants, and will render vengeance to his adversaries, and will be merciful unto his land, and to his people.

(44) And Moses came and spoke all the words of this song in the ears of the people, he, and Hoshea the son of Nun.

This is the song of Moses; better learn it if you expect God to welcome you into his Kingdom.

Revelation 15:5-8

(4) Who shall not fear thee, O Lord, and glorify thy name? for thou only art holy: for all nations shall come and worship before thee; for thy judgments are made manifest.

(5) And after that I looked, and behold, the temple of the tabernacle of the testimony in heaven was opened:

(6) And the seven angels came out of the temple, having the seven plagues, clothed in pure and white linen, and having their breasts girded with golden girdles.

(7) And one of the four beasts gave unto the seven angels seven golden vials full of the wrath of God, who lives for ever and ever.

(8) And the temple was filled with smoke from the glory of God, and from his power; and no man was able to enter into the temple, till the seven plagues of the seven angels were fulfilled.

The fat lady is about to sing; it's almost over. These last seven vials will finish destroying the enemies of God. Noticed, I said the enemies of God; if you're standing right in the middle of all the coming turmoil and belong to God, none of the contents of these vials will harm you. They are just for God's enemies.

Revelation 16:1-21

(1) And I heard a great voice out of the temple saying to the seven angels, go your ways, and pour out the vials of the wrath of God upon the earth.

(2) And the first went and poured out his vial upon the earth; and there fell a noisome and grievous sore upon the men which had the mark of the beast, and upon them which worshipped his image.

Like I said, only the ones who have the mark of the Beast; that is, followers of Satan.

(3) And the second angel poured out his vial upon the sea; and it became as the blood of a dead man: and every living soul died in the sea.

Always keep in mind, the waters or sea are symbolic of people. When the flesh dies, the soul returns to God and in this case the souls are placed across the 'vast gulf' where the 'rich man' and other enemies of God await their judgment.

(4) And the third angel poured out his vial upon the rivers and fountains of waters; and they became blood.

(5) And I heard the angel of the waters say, thou art righteous, O Lord, which art, and was, and shalt be, because thou hast judged thus.

(6) For they have shed the blood of saints and prophets, and thou hast given them blood to drink; for they are worthy.

(7) And I heard another out of the altar say, even so, Lord God Almighty, true, and righteous are thy judgments.

What does the sun remind you of? Sun worshippers or the ones indoctrinated into the Catholic Church and the same heathen religion started way back in the days of Nimrod. The only thing changed from then until now is the name. Think of all the people who this fake church killed during the inquisition?

(8) And the fourth angel poured out his vial upon the sun; and power was given unto him to scorch men with fire.

(9) And men were scorched with great heat, and blasphemed the name of God, which hath power over

these plagues: and they repented not to give him glory.

Even when the Papacy was scorched, they wouldn't repent of their actions, instead they cursed God. This is nothing new; take a look at the same thing is Ezekiel's day. Look at Ezekiel 8:14-16

(14) Then he brought me to the door of the gate of the LORD'S house which was toward the north; and behold, there sat women weeping for Tammuz.

(15) Then said he unto me, Hast thou seen this, O son of man? turn thee yet again, and thou shalt see greater abominations than these.

(16) And he brought me into the inner court of the LORD'S house, and behold, at the door of the temple of the LORD, between the porch and the altar, were about five and twenty men, with their backs toward the temple of the LORD, and their faces toward the east; and they worshipped the sun toward the east.

Revelation 16:10

(10) And the fifth angel poured out his vial upon the seat of the beast; and his kingdom was full of darkness; and they gnawed their tongues for pain,

(11) And blasphemed the God of heaven because of their pains and their sores and repented not of their deeds.

Still clinging to the church; even though it's Satan's church.

(12) And the sixth angel poured out his vial upon the great river Euphrates; and the water thereof was dried up, that the way of the kings of the east might be prepared.

(13) And I saw three unclean spirits like frogs come out of the mouth of the dragon, and out of the mouth of the beast, and out of the mouth of the false prophet

(14) For they are the spirits of devils, working miracles, which go forth unto the kings of the earth and of the whole world, to gather them to the battle of that great day of God Almighty.

(15) Behold, I come as a thief. Blessed is he that watches, and keeps his garments, lest he walk naked, and they see his shame.

(16) And he gathered them together into a place called in the Hebrew tongue Armageddon.

Who is the dragon, the Beast, the false prophet? This is Satan's bunch. What are they doing? They are working miracles, conning everybody who followers them into believing an alien attack or something like it is about to destroy their world. What does Armageddon translate into English? Simple; the gathering place of the crowd. They are coming to fight against Christ and his saved ones. Who do you think will win?

(17) And the seventh angel poured out his vial into the air; and there came a great voice out of the temple of heaven, from the throne, saying, it is done.

(18) And there were voices, and thunders, and lightnings; and there was a great earthquake, such as

was not since men were upon the earth, so mighty an earthquake, and so great.

(19) And the great city was divided into three parts, and the cities of the nation's fell: and great Babylon came in remembrance before God, to give unto her the cup of the wine of the fierceness of his wrath.

(20) And every island fled away, and the mountains were not found.

(21) And there fell upon men a great hail out of heaven, every stone about the weight of a talent: and men blasphemed God because of the plague of the hail; for the plague thereof was exceeding great.

It's too late; it's all over. Christ has returned and everybody living is instantly changed into a spiritual body.

Zechariah 14:4,

(4) And his feet shall stand in that day upon the mount of Olives, which is before Jerusalem on the east, and the mount of Olives shall cleave in the midst

thereof toward the east and toward the west, and there shall be a very great valley; and half of the mountain shall remove toward the north, and half of it toward the south.

Zechariah 14:12

(12) And this shall be the plague wherewith the LORD will smite all the people that have fought against Jerusalem; Their flesh shall consume away while they stand upon their feet, and their eyes shall consume away in their holes, and their tongue shall consume away in their mouth.

Zechariah 14:9

(9) And the LORD shall be king over all the earth: in that day shall there be one LORD, and his name one.

It's all over but the shouting. Christ has been crowned King of this world and now he will bring judgment to the one who fought against him.

Revelation 17:1-7

(1) And there came one of the seven angels which had the seven vials, and talked with me, saying unto me, come hither; I will shew unto thee the judgment of the great whore that sited upon many waters:

(2) With whom the kings of the earth have committed fornication, and the inhabitants of the earth have been made drunk with the wine of her fornication.

(3) So, he carried me away in the spirit into the wilderness: and I saw a woman sit upon a scarlet-colored beast, full of names of blasphemy, having seven heads and ten horns.

(4) And the woman was arrayed in purple and scarlet color and decked with gold and precious stones and pearls, having a golden cup in her hand full of abominations and filthiness of her fornication:

(5) And upon her forehead was a name written, MYSTERY, BABYLON THE GREAT, THE MOTHER OF HARLOTS AND ABOMINATIONS OF THE EARTH.

(6) And I saw the woman drunken with the blood of the saints, and with the blood of the martyrs

of Jesus: and when I saw her, I wondered with great admiration.

(7) And the angel said unto me, wherefore didst thou marvel? I will tell thee the mystery of the woman, and of the beast that carried her, which hath the seven heads and ten horns.

Who is the great whore? First, I think you should know what or who is considered a whore. By the English dictionary, a whore is a person who charges for favors of one kind or another: usually sexual. Some synonyms given are, a prostitute, promiscuous woman, slut, sex worker, call girl, white slave, etc. An organization or political party, or a religious group could also fit this scenario. So now let's look at the 'great whore' given in Revelation 17:1-7

The 1st verse informs us God is about to judge the great whore and the 2nd verse let's us know the kings of the earth have committed fornication with her.

The kings of the earth, you remember, are Political, finance, government, and religion. And what else; the people have been made drunk with her ideas and teachings and fornication.

John was carried away in the spirit into a wilderness and what did he see; a woman arrayed in gold and precious stones and pearls having a golden cup filled with abominations and filthiness. She was dressed in purple, the color of royalty, and had a name written across her forehead, MYSTERY BABYLON THE GREAT, MOTHER OF HARLOTS AND ABOMINATIONS OF THE EARTH. She was drunk with the blood of saints and martyrs of Jesus Christ.

Revelation 17:8-18

(8) The beast that thou sawest was and is not; and shall ascend out of the bottomless pit and go into perdition: and they that dwell on the earth shall wonder, whose names were not written in the book of

life from the foundation of the world, when they behold the beast that was, and is not, and yet is.

SATAN!!

(9) And here is the mind which hath wisdom. The seven heads are seven mountains, on which the woman sits.

I heard about the 7 hills of Rome most of my life; but this not what this verse means. Mountains are symbolic of kingdoms. Theses kingdoms are basically the Nations of Europe today. These are the descendants of the tribes which migrated across the Caucasus Mountains from Israel after the Assyrian Empire was defeated by the Babylonians under Nebuchadnezzar. Theses Mountains or Nations started out as 10 countries but 3 were dissolved by the Papacy. The ones lost are the Heruli, the Vandals, Ostrogoths; they disagreed with the teachings of the Catholic Church and were a threat to the power of the

Papacy, so these three were eliminated. This agrees with the book of Daniel, chapter seven, verse eight:

(8) I considered the horns, and behold, there came up among them another little horn, before whom there were three of the first horns plucked up by the roots: and behold, in this horn were eyes like the eyes of man, and a mouth speaking great things.

In the book of Daniel, these tribes are called 'horns' meaning power. They have not become Kings as yet and the little horn is the Papacy; it has not received great power as yet, either.

Continuing with Revelation 17:10

(10) And there are seven kings: five are fallen, and one is, and the other is not yet come; and when he cometh, he must continue a short space.

(11) And the beast that was, and is not, even he is the eighth, and is of the seven, and goes into perdition.

Who are the five kings which have fallen? I say, the first was Nimrod, who started this mystery religion with his wife Semiramis, the second, Nebuchadnezzar; the third, the Medo-Persian; the fourth, Alexander and the Greek Empire; the fifth, Roman Empire; the sixth and still functioning, the Papacy of the Catholic Church. They all have one thing in common; they are ruled by Satan. Which brings us to the seventh; who is he? I say none other then Satan himself, playing the role of the Christ. He will be removed when the real Christ returns to earth and this phony will be cast into the 'bottomless pit'. God will release him after the thousand-year period of Christ's teachers and priest have finished their work. This is done to sort the sheep from the goats; that is, the true followers of Christ from the ones who cling to Satan's way of life. After Satan is released from the 'bottomless pit', he will gather together his followers and they will attack Christ. After this takes place, our Heavenly Father will say, enough is enough and he will cast Satan and his bunch into the 'lake of fire'.

(12) And the ten horns which thou sawest are ten kings, which have received no kingdom as yet; but receive power as kings one hour with the beast.

(13) These have one mind and shall give their power and strength unto the beast.

(14) These shall make war with the Lamb, and the Lamb shall overcome them: for he is Lord of lords, and King of kings: and they that are with him are called, and chosen, and faithful.

(15) And he saith unto me, the waters which thou sawest, where the whore sits, are peoples, and multitudes, and nations, and tongues.

(16) And the ten horns which thou sawest upon the beast, these shall hate the whore, and shall make her desolate and naked, and shall eat her flesh, and burn her with fire.

(17) For God hath put in their hearts to fulfil his will, and to agree, and give their kingdom unto the beast, until the words of God shall be fulfilled.

(18) And the woman which thou sawest is that great city, which reigns over the kings of the earth.

The great city is the Vatican, hiding inside the city of Rome. In the next chapter, it is called Babylon; it called Babylon because the Vatican hadn't been named at this writing of John. Don't forget who or what the kings of the earth are! Here is a reminder; political, financial, commerce, and religion.

Chapter 14

Revelation 18:1-24

(1) And after these things I saw another angel come down from heaven, having great power; and the earth was lightened with his glory.

(2) And he cried mightily with a strong voice, saying, Babylon the great is fallen, is fallen, and is become the habitation of devils, and the hold of every foul spirit, and a cage of every unclean and hateful bird.

Who is this angel coming down from heaven? Could it be our Christ returning as he said he would?

And his message is, 'Babylon' is fallen; Babylon translated into English is 'babble' or 'confusion'. How can confusion be gone from the world; unless, Christ has returned, and everybody has been changed into their spiritual bodies? This being the case, the rest of the verses make sense. In your spiritual body, you'll have no need of anything physical, gold, silver, precious stones, material wealth of any kind will have no value. The 'kings' of the earth, 'political, education, commerce, religion,' will not be needed in a spiritual body.

(3) For all nations have drunk of the wine of the wrath of her fornication, and the kings of the earth have committed fornication with her, and the merchants of the earth are waxed rich through the abundance of her delicacies.

(4) And I heard another voice from heaven, saying, come out of her, my people, that ye be not partakers of her sins, and that ye receive not of her plagues.

(5) For her sins have reached unto heaven, and
God hath remembered her iniquities.

(6) Reward her even as she rewarded you, and
double unto her double according to her works: in the
cup which she hath filled fill to her double.

(7) How much she hath glorified herself, and
lived deliciously, so much torment and sorrow give
her: for she saith in her heart, I sit a queen, and am
no widow, and shall see no sorrow.

(8) Therefore, shall her plagues come in one
day, death, and mourning, and famine; and she shall
be utterly burned with fire: for strong is the Lord God
who judges her.

(9) And the kings of the earth, who have
committed fornication and lived deliciously with her,
shall bewail her, and lament for her, when they shall
see the smoke of her burning,

(10) Standing afar off for the fear of her
torment, saying, Alas, alas, that great city Babylon,
that mighty city! for in one hour is thy judgment
come.

It started with Nimrod and Semiramis and their 'mystery religion' and has ended with the Papacy. The name of this religious cult has changed many times, but the message is still the same; honor men and material things instead of our Heavenly Father who owns everything.

(11) And the merchants of the earth shall weep and mourn over her; for no man buys their merchandise anymore:

(12) The merchandise of gold, and silver, and precious stones, and of pearls, and fine linen, and purple, and silk, and scarlet, and all thyine wood, and all manner vessels of ivory, and all manner vessels of most precious wood, and of brass, and iron, and marble,

(13) And cinnamon, and odors, and ointments, and frankincense, and wine, and oil, and fine flour, and wheat, and beasts, and sheep, and horses, and chariots, and slaves, and souls of men.

(14) And the fruits that thy soul lusted after are departed from thee, and all things which were dainty and goodly are departed from thee, and thou shalt find them no more at all.

(15) The merchants of these things, which were made rich by her, shall stand afar off for the fear of her torment, weeping and wailing,

(16) And saying, Alas, alas, that great city, that was clothed in fine linen, and purple, and scarlet, and decked with gold, and precious stones, and pearls!

(17) For in one hour so great riches are come to naught. And every shipmaster, and all the company in ships, and sailors, and as many as trade by sea, stood afar off,

(18) And cried when they saw the smoke of her burning, saying, what city is like unto this great city!

(19) And they cast dust on their heads, and cried, weeping, and wailing, saying, Alas, alas, that great city, wherein were made rich all that had ships in the sea by reason of her costliness! for in one hour is she made desolate.

(20) Rejoice over her, thou heaven, and ye holy apostles and prophets; for God hath avenged you on her.

(21) And a mighty angel took up a stone like a great millstone, and cast it into the sea, saying, thus with violence shall that great city Babylon be thrown down, and shall be found no more at all.

(22) And the voice of harpers, and musicians, and of pipers, and trumpeters, shall be heard no more at all in thee; and no craftsman, of whatsoever craft he be, shall be found any more in thee; and the sound of a millstone shall be heard no more at all in thee.

(23) And the light of a candle shall shine no more at all in thee; and the voice of the bridegroom and of the bride shall be heard no more at all in thee: for thy merchants were the great men of the earth; for by thy sorceries were all nations deceived.

(24) And in her was found the blood of prophets, and of saints, and of all that were slain upon the earth.

Revelation 19;1-21

(1) And after these things I heard a great voice of many people in heaven, saying, Alleluia, Salvation, and glory, and honor, and power, unto the Lord our God:

The first six verses of this chapter are praises for our Lord God and for all he has done for his believers.

Next, we come to the marriage of the Lamb. This marriage takes place between God's true church and not the fake one supported by Satan. We see Christ and his followers ride forth in a pure white linen wardrobe signifying purity and perfection.

Next, we are shown an angel calling for the birds of the heavens to come and eat the flesh of kings, horses, mighty men, and all flesh. Why would the angel call the birds to do this? The reason is simple; when Christ returns, all flesh dies that walk the earth. The ones who have a spirit placed in them by God, releases the spirit the moment the flesh dies. There will be a lot of rotting, stinking flesh left all over the earth unless something cleans it up. The birds will do this.

Revelation 19:17-18

(17) And I saw an angel standing in the sun; and he cried with a loud voice, saying to all the fowls that fly in the midst of heaven, Come, and gather yourselves together unto the supper of the great God.

(18) That ye may eat the flesh of kings, and the flesh of captains, and the flesh of mighty men, and the flesh of horses, and of them that sit on them, and the flesh of all men, both free and bond, both small and great.

After this, the beast and the kings of the earth gather to make war against Christ and his army. The beast was taken, and the false prophet and they were cast alive into 'lake of fire' burning with brimstone. Then their followers were slain with the sword of Christ. Don't get upset at the violence of what is taking place; the beast and false prophet are ideas Satan has deceived the world using them.

Revelation 19:20-21

(20) And the beast was taken, and with him the false prophet that wrought miracles before him, with which he deceived them that had received the mark of the beast, and them that worshipped his image. These both were cast alive into a lake of fire burning with brimstone.

(21) And the remnant was slain with the sword of him that sat upon the horse, which sword proceeded out of his mouth: and all the fowls were filled with their flesh.

Revelation 20:1-3

(1) And I saw an angel come down from heaven, having the key to the bottomless pit and a great chain in his hand.

(2) And he laid hold on the dragon, that old serpent, which is the Devil, and Satan, and bound him a thousand years,

(3) And cast him into the bottomless pit, and shut him up, and set a seal upon him, that he should deceive the nations no more, till the thousand years

should be fulfilled: and after that he must be loosed a little season.

We are finally through with the Devil and his deception; or at least, for a thousand years. He has been captured and bound with a chain and placed in a bottomless pit and sealed up. How long? A thousand years. And then he's going to be released for a spell. Why would God release him, knowing all he has done?

Do you remember all the ones who were deceived by the Devil and have been taught God's way of doing things? Well, now God wants to know if they have learned their lesson and will they stay true to our Heavenly Father though out eternality. The only way he can know for sure is to have them tested, and what better way to do this than by releasing their leader from prison and see if they will follow him again or not. Sad to say, but a great multitude will still worship the devil.

Revelation 20:7-9

(7) And when the thousand years are expired, Satan shall be loosed out of his prison,

(8) And shall go out to deceive the nations which are in the four quarters of the earth, Gog, and Magog, to gather them together to battle: the number of whom is as the sand of the sea.

(9) And they went up on the breadth of the earth, and compassed the camp of the saints about, and the beloved city: and fire came down from God out of heaven and devoured them.

(10) And the devil that deceived them was cast into the lake of fire and brimstone, where the beast and the false prophet are, and shall be tormented day and night for ever and ever.

How many still followed the Devil? The number was as the 'sand of the sea'; sad isn't it?

Are we through with Satan now? Yes, he's gone forever. The once beautiful angel of God who was bestowed the role of Cherub, to help guard the mercy seat of God is finally destroyed because he rebelled against the government of God and felt he should be God. Don't make this same mistake people!

Revelation 20:12-15

(12) And I saw the dead, small and great, stand before God; and the books were opened: and another book was opened, which is the book of life: and the dead were judged out of those things which were written in the books, according to their works.

(13) And the sea gave up the dead which were in it; and death and hell delivered up the dead which were in them: and they were judged every man according to their works.

(14) And death and hell were cast into the lake of fire. This is the second death.

(15) And whosoever was not found written in the book of life was cast into the lake of fire.

Revelation 21:1-6

(1) And I saw a new heaven and a new earth: for the first heaven and the first earth were passed away; and there was no more sea. (no more flesh people)

(2) And I John saw the holy city, new Jerusalem, coming down from God out of heaven, prepared as a bride adorned for her husband. (This is the Holy City, new Jerusalem, as stated in Matthew 27:52-53)

(3) And I heard a great voice out of heaven saying, Behold, the tabernacle of God is with men, and he will dwell with them, and they shall be his people, and God himself shall be with them, and be their God.

(4) And God shall wipe away all tears from their eyes; and there shall be no more death, neither sorrow, nor crying, neither shall there be any more pain: for the former things are passed away.

(5) And he that sat upon the throne said, Behold, I make all things new. And he said unto me, write for these words are true and faithful.

(6) And he said unto me, it is done. I am "Alpha and Omega", the beginning and the end. I will give unto him that is athirst of the fountain of the water of life freely.

Everybody is now in a spiritual body; one that doesn't age or get sick any more forever. All the ones who didn't like our Heavenly Father or the way he did things or live a life enjoying the things God has created for us no more exist. They have all been wiped out in the Lake of Fire.

What is the Lake of Fire, you might wonder? It is our God, or our Heavenly Father. He is the one who created all things, and it was done by Christ.

Hebrews 12:29

(29) For our God is a consuming fire.

Rev. 21:7-8

(7) He that overcomes shall inherit all things; and I will be his God, and he shall be my son.

(8) But the fearful, and unbelieving, and the abominable, and murderers, and whoremongers, and sorcerers, and idolaters, and all liars, shall have their part in the lake which burns with fire and brimstone: which is the second death.

God gives a list of the things which displeases him. If this is your lifestyle and you don't see any need to repent of this type of lifestyle and you won't accept Christ as your King, you will not be in Heaven at this time, you will have already been consumed in the lake of fire.

Rev. 21:9-10

(9) And there came unto me one of the seven angels which had the seven vials full of the seven last plagues, and talked with me, saying, come hither, I will shew thee the bride, the Lamb's wife.

(10) And he carried me away in the spirit to a great and high mountain, and shewed me that great city, the holy Jerusalem, descending out of heaven from God,

Did you know God has a wife? In reading the above verses, did you catch who or what is the wife of God. From what I read, the Lamb's bride or wife is the 'New Jerusalem' descending out of heaven from God.

The rest of this chapter gives a beautiful description of the New Jerusalem, and a little bit about the function of the city.

Rev. 21:11-21

(11) Having the glory of God: and her light was like unto a stone most precious, even like a jasper stone, clear as crystal.

(12) And had a wall great and high, and had twelve gates, and at the gates twelve angels, and names written thereon, which are the names of the twelve tribes of the children of Israel:

(13) On the east three gates; on the north three gates; on the south three gates; and on the west three gates.

(14) And the wall of the city had twelve foundations, and in them the names of the twelve apostles of the Lamb.

(15) And he that talked with me had a golden reed to measure the city, and the gates thereof, and the wall thereof.

(16) And the city lieth foursquare, and the length is as large as the breadth: and he measured the city with the reed, twelve thousand furlongs. The length and the breadth and the height of it are equal.

(17) And he measured the wall thereof, a hundred and forty and four cubits, according to the measure of a man, that is, of the angel.

(18) And the building of the wall of it was of jasper: and the city was pure gold, like unto clear glass.

(19) And the foundations of the wall of the city were garnished with all manner of precious stones. The first foundation was jasper; the second, sapphire; the third, a chalcedony; the fourth, an emerald.

(20) The fifth, sardonyx; the sixth, sardius; the seventh, chrysolite; the eighth, beryl; the ninth, a

topaz; the tenth, a chrysoprasus; the eleventh, a jacinth; the twelfth, an amethyst.

(21) And the twelve gates were twelve pearls; every several gates were of one pearl: and the street of the city was pure gold, as it were transparent glass.

Did you understand the size of this New Jerusalem? It is a cube, and the length, breath, and height are the same and it is 1500 miles on a side. I think there will be enough room in it for all God's children. Don't you?

Rev.21:22-27

(22) And I saw no temple therein: for the Lord God Almighty and the Lamb are the temple of it.

(23) And the city had no need of the sun, neither of the moon, to shine in it: for the glory of God did lighten it, and the Lamb is the light thereof.

(24) And the nations of them which are saved shall walk in the light of it: and the kings of the earth do bring their glory and honor into it.

(25) And the gates of it shall not be shut at all by day: for there shall be no night there.

(26) And they shall bring the glory and honor of the nations into it.

(27) And there shall in no wise enter into it anything that defiles, neither whatsoever worketh abomination, or makes a lie: but they which are written in the Lamb's book of life.

Chapter 15

(1) And he shewed me a pure river of water of life, clear as crystal, proceeding out of the throne of God and of the Lamb.

(2) In the midst of the street of it, and on either side of the river, was there the tree of life, which bare twelve manner of fruits, and yielded her fruit every month: and the leaves of the tree were for the healing of the nations.

(3) And there shall be no more curse: but the throne of God and of the Lamb shall be in it; and his servants shall serve him:

(4) And they shall see his face; and his name shall be in their foreheads.

(5) And there shall be no night there; and they need no candle, neither light of the sun; for the Lord God giveth them light: and they shall reign for ever and ever.

(6) And he said unto me, these sayings are faithful and true: and the Lord God of the holy prophets sent his angel to shew unto his servants the things which must shortly be done.

(7) Behold, I come quickly: blessed is he that keeps the sayings of the prophecy of this book.

(8) And I John saw these things and heard them. And when I had heard and seen, I fell down to

worship before the feet of the angel which shewed me these things.

(9) Then saith he unto me, see thou do it not: for I am thy fellow servant, and of thy brethren the prophets, and of them which keep the sayings of this book: worship God.

(10) And he saith unto me, Seal not the sayings of the prophecy of this book: for the time is at hand.

(11) He that is unjust, let him be unjust still: and he which is filthy, let him be filthy still: and he that is righteous, let him be righteous still: and he that is holy, let him be holy still.

(12) And behold, I come quickly; and my reward is with me, to give every man according as his work shall be.

(13) I am Alpha and Omega, the beginning, and the end, the first and the last.

(14) Blessed are they that do his commandments, that they may have right to the tree of life and may enter in through the gates into the city.

(15) For without are dogs, and sorcerers, and whoremongers, and murderers, and idolaters, and whosoever loveth and makes a lie.

(16) I Jesus have sent mine angel to testify unto you these things in the churches. I am the root and the offspring of David, and the bright and morning star.

(17) And the Spirit and the bride say, Come. And let him that heareth say, Come. And let him that is athirst come. And whosoever will, let him take the water of life freely.

(18) For I testify unto every man that heareth the words of the prophecy of this book, if any man

shall add unto these things, God shall add unto him the plagues that are written in this book:

(19) And if any man shall take away from the words of the book of this prophecy, God shall take away his part out of the book of life, and out of the holy city, and from the things which are written in this book.

(20) He which testifies these things saith, surely, I come quickly. Amen. Even so, come, Lord Jesus.

(21) The grace of our Lord Jesus Christ be with you all. Amen.

I think this last chapter is fairly self-explanatory. I see no reason for me to make a comment.

1 Thessalonians 4:13-17

(13) But I would not have you to be ignorant, brethren, concerning them which are asleep, that ye sorrow not, even as others which have no hope.

(asleep = dead)

(14) For if we believe that Jesus died and rose again, even so them also which sleep in Jesus will God bring with him.

(15) For this we say unto you by the word of the Lord, that we which are alive and remain unto the coming of the Lord shall not prevent them which are asleep.

(We can't prevent (go first) them because they are already with Christ.)

(16) For the Lord himself shall descend from heaven with a shout, with the voice of the archangel, and with the trump of God: and the dead in Christ shall rise first:

(Dead in Christ will arise first because they have already risen; when the flesh body dies, the spirit immediately returns to God who gave it. Eccl. 12:7)

(17) Then we which are alive and remain shall be caught up together with them in the clouds, to meet the Lord in the air: and so, shall we ever be with the Lord.

This word air is translated from the Greek word AER, and it means air alright, but do you know what kind of air Paul was talking about? There are 3 or 4 Greek words which translate to Air. This Greek word, AER, translated air is referring to the air in your lungs. Nothing more! Will we meet Christ in his lungs or maybe God's lungs; don't be ridiculous. As used here, it means in the spirit!

This is the way it will be the day our Savior returns. It won't be as some preach a fly-away doctrine. Of course, God tells us he is against those who misled his children teaching a fly away doctrine.

Ezekiel 13:20

(20) Wherefore thus saith the Lord GOD;
Behold, I am against your pillows, wherewith ye there
hunt the souls to make them fly, and I will tear them
from your arms, and will let the souls go, even the
souls that ye hunt to make them fly.

Zechariah 14:1-4

(1) Behold, the day of the LORD cometh, and
thy spoil shall be divided in the midst of thee.

(2) For I will gather all nations against
Jerusalem to battle; and the city shall be taken, and
the houses rifled, and the women ravished; and half
of the city shall go forth into captivity, and the residue
of the people shall not be cut off from the city.

(3) Then shall the LORD go forth, and fight
against those nations, as when he fought in the day of
battle.

(4) And his feet shall stand in that day upon the
mount of Olives, which is before Jerusalem on the
east, and the mount of Olives shall cleave in the midst

thereof toward the east and toward the west, and there shall be a very great valley; and half of the mountain shall remove toward the north, and half of it toward the south.

The day of the Lord; the day all Christians have been waiting for 2000 years, give or take. Are you happy? You should be, it doesn't matter whether you had the scriptures right or wrong. Christ is not mad at you, he's mad at Satan and his bunch who have deceived his children for so many centuries.

Mr. Hathcock is a graduate of Almeda University with a master's degree in Religious Theology. He has written several books on misunderstood issues concerning the English translations of God's written word. He has been married to Katherine Hathcock for 49 years and they have two children and three grandchildren. He lives in the Anderson area and has been there for 33 years. He can be reached at his e-mail address: DavidHath@msn.com or by letter at 1751 Welcome Rd. Williamston, SC 29697

Mr. Hathcock has several books available for purchase. They are "A Path Thru the Weeds"; "The Way of Cain"; "he touched me"; "The Eternal Purpose" and several more, including "We Are Warriors" and "Tumbleweed". These can be ordered from David Hathcock from email 'davidhath@msn.com'. or thru Amazon's bookstore.

Numerous pamphlets and articles dealing with misrepresented subjected are available from Mr.

Hathcock by contacting him through his e-mail address. They are free upon request. Mr. Hathcock will lecture at your meeting place on biblical issues; discussing the truths of God's word, if requested.